ANTIQUE CAR MODELS

Other Books by Frank Ross, Jr.

ANTIQUE CAR MODELS

THEIR STORIES AND HOW TO MAKE THEM

FRANK ROSS JR.

illustrated with diagrams by the author and photographs by
George A. Haddad

Lothrop, Lee & Shepard Co.

A Division of William Morrow & Company
New York

Copyright © 1978 by Frank Ross, Jr.
All rights reserved. No part of this book may be reproduced or
utilized in any form or by any means, electronic or mechanical,
including photocopying, recording or by any information storage
and retrieval system, without permission in writing from the
Publisher. Inquiries should be addressed to Lothrop, Lee &
Shepard Company, 105 Madison Ave., New York, N.Y. 10016.

Printed in the United States of America.

First Edition
1   2   3   4   5   6   7   8   9   10

Library of Congress Cataloging in Publication Data

Ross, Frank Xavier (date)
  Antique car models, their stories and how to make them.
  Includes index.
  1. Automobiles—Models.   I. Haddad, George A.   II. Title.
TL237.R66   629.22'1'22   78-2349
ISBN 0-688-41833-3
ISBN 0-688-51833-8 lib. bdg.

Contents

For **Dode Hulse** With Best Wishes

Introduction

Today antique cars have an enormous appeal for thousands of hobbyists and collectors. Their design seems colorful and unique, especially when compared to modern sleek cars. Some hobbyists are also attracted to antique cars by the challenge of tracking down and restoring an old relic of bygone years. For others, it may be the appeal of victory in a cross-country competition, or of winning top honors for the best restored old car. Almost all feel nostalgia for the simple, charming vehicles produced during the automobile's early years. Whatever the reason, antique car collectors pursue their hobby with an enthusiasm that is hard to match.

This is a book mainly for model-making hobbyists, especially those with a love for antique cars. The four typical old cars chosen for the models in this book are of special interest to car buffs. Not only are they reminders of the motor car's colorful, adventure-filled past, but they also represent the three most common forms of early automotive power—steam, electricity, and the gasoline-burning internal combustion engine. In addition, they reveal the rapid changes in exterior design during the automobile's early years.

In the late 1800s and early 1900s when motor cars first began appearing in large numbers, they had a strong resemblance to the horse-drawn carriages they were rapidly replacing. The Curved Dash Olds of 1902, which leads off the series of models, clearly shows its carriage heritage. By 1915, the automobile had acquired its own distinctive appearance which can be seen in the Chevrolet, the final model described in this book.

After building these models, you may be curious to see what

they and other antique cars actually looked like. There are a number of museums you can visit both in this country and Europe with extensive, fascinating automobile collections. A few of the best in the United States are the Henry Ford Museum, Dearborn, Michigan; Museum of Science and Industry, Jackson Park, Chicago, Illinois; and the Smithsonian Institution, Washington, D.C.

Of course, your cardboard-and-construction-paper antique car models will not be exact miniatures of the real vehicles. Nevertheless, the challenge of building these replicas can be as enjoyable and satisfying as restoring a real antique car. You may find the history and construction of these four models fascinating enough to inspire you to create other models of your own design. Whether your goal is a real Model T Ford in your garage or a display case filled with your car models, the four antique cars in this book are sure to give you hours of creator's enjoyment and years of builder's pride.

Materials and Tools

For making your antique car models, select a sturdy work surface with a flat, smooth top. Cover it with a sheet of strong paper, which will protect it from accidental glue spills and knife scratches. Oaktag, available at many stationery or art and craft supply stores, is good for this purpose. Try to use a light-colored paper, which will keep tools and materials easily visible as you work on a model.

If possible, work on a table that you can use until the model is complete. Then you won't have to put away your tools and materials after every work session.

The following materials and tools are necessary for making the models in this book.

MATERIALS

Construction paper—Construction paper, like the kind used in school art classes, is ideal for making these models because it comes in a variety of colors, bends easily, and glues very well. Most important, perhaps, it will make your finished models look much more attractive than if you used pieces of scrap paper. You can find reasonably priced construction paper at paint shops that have art supplies departments, stationery stores, and hobby or craft shops.

Rigid cardboard—You can find excellent rigid cardboard from boxes around the house. Empty shoe boxes are the perfect thickness for making the models in this book. Empty cereal boxes are not as good as shoe boxes, but they can be made rigid enough by gluing together two or three pieces of cereal box material.

A box made of several layers of compressed paper, like a cigar box, is very good for making parts such as wheels and chassis. Ask owners of stores where cigars are sold if you may have their empty boxes.

As a last resort, you may also buy rigid cardboard in sheets. Matting board, often used for framing pictures, is an inexpensive cardboard, and is easy to draw on and cut. You can find matting board in art supply stores and some well-stocked camera shops.

Whatever rigid cardboard you decide to use for the models in this book, be sure it does not have a shiny surface. Glue does not absorb well or stick properly to a slick surface. It is also difficult to draw on a shiny surface with pen and ink or crayon. Whenever shiny-surface cardboard is suggested in the following pages, the material is used only as a surface on which to assemble and glue parts of the model. It is never used to make sections of the models themselves.

Drinking straws—Large or jumbo-size drinking straws are the best kind to use for building the antique car models. If you don't have these around the house and need to buy them, choose the plainest straws you can find. Too much decoration makes it difficult to paint the straws.

Wooden matchsticks—For making axles and steering posts, the wood of extra-long matches (commonly used for starting fires in fireplaces) is ideal. You can buy these matches in most hardware stores. For your own safety, be sure to remove the flammable tips of the matches before working with the wood.

Round toothpicks—Round, not flat, toothpicks are used to make brake handles, lamp decorations, and crank handles, and to construct roof frames for the car models. Usually only the thick, center portion of the toothpick is needed. Flat toothpicks are too weak for car-model building.

Cotton thread—Black cotton thread, about six inches long, is needed for making the windshield of the 1915 Chevrolet.

India ink, crayon, and poster paints—These are used to draw various designs on the wheels and bodies of the cars, and to color many of the parts. Although you may choose other colors, black, yellow, and orange are the only ink and paint colors suggested for the four car models. The smallest size ink and paint containers (1 ounce) are all you'll need. Recommended brands are Grumbacher, Koh-i-noor, Pelikan, and Higgins. The only color crayon needed is black.

Wire—About seventeen inches of paper-covered wire is needed to make the seat rail for the Curved Dash Olds of 1902. Do not try to use the plastic-coated kind instead, since it will not absorb the glue and stick properly. Paper-coated wire is often used for making artificial flowers, and can be purchased from art supply stores or craft materials shops.

TOOLS

Scissors—A pair of strong, sharp scissors for cutting construction paper and cardboard parts is the most important tool for building these antique car models. For smaller, more complex parts, a small, straight cuticle scissors is helpful.

Knife—A sharp knife is the next most important tool. It is used for cutting the lengths and angles of the various wooden parts, and for scoring the construction paper. To score, run the point of the knife once or twice along the line marking the fold edge. Scoring will give you a straighter, cleaner fold.

Although you can use any small knife with a good point and cutting edge, an X-acto knife, made especially for model-making and artwork, is excellent. However, when scoring paper with an X-acto knife, you must be extra careful to press lightly so that the blade does not cut the paper.

Glue—White glue, such as Elmer's Glue-All or Sobo, is needed to attach the various parts of the car models. Whatever brand you choose, be sure it dries quickly and sticks well to paper and wood. A 4-ounce bottle is enough to make all the models in this book.

Pencils—For measuring and drawing the different parts of the models, it is useful to have a medium-soft (No. 2½) pencil.

Ruler—A 12-inch, metal-edge ruler for measuring and drawing straight lines is needed for building all the antique car models.

Hammer—If you can, borrow a hammer from the family toolbox. It is useful for tapping the back of your knife when cutting the various lengths of matchstick and toothpick wood needed for the car parts.

Compass—Since there are a lot of circular parts to the antique car models, a good compass is essential.

Tweezers—Unless you are able to hold small pieces quite easily, you will find a pair of tweezers a must for these models.

Drawing pen—For making the designs on the car models, you will need a pen with black drawing ink or any black felt-tip pen.

Masking tape—Use small pieces of masking tape to hold your construction paper to your work surface while you draw the patterns or designs.

Nail—A sharp-pointed nail is extremely handy for making holes in various parts of the car models.

Block of wood—To prevent damage to your work surface, a small block of wood is helpful as a base for cutting matchsticks or toothpicks.

Plastic curve—This draftsman's tool is useful for drawing the curves of many of the car model parts.

Paintbrush—A small brush is needed for painting many of the car model parts.

General Directions

The antique car models whose construction is described in this book represent the three common forms of motor power used in early automobiles. These were the internal combustion engine using gasoline fuel (Curved Dash Olds of 1902 and Chevrolet of 1915); the electric power unit (Waverley Stanhope Electric of 1909); and steam power (Stanley Steamer of 1911).

Although the models are described in chronological order, you may build them in any sequence you wish. No one model is easier or more difficult to make than any other. In fact, you will find that there are identically constructed parts, such as wheel boxes, which are used on all four car models. After you have made two or three models, these repeated parts should become easier to construct and more attractive as your model-making skills improve.

The following general instructions will help you with some of the more difficult construction methods and will add to your model-making enjoyment.

1. Skim through the book before you start building any of the car models. When you have decided which one to build first, read the directions for it carefully to be sure you understand all the steps. Do the same for each model you build. Before you begin, gather your materials and tools, and select construction paper and paint in the color you want for your antique car model.

2. To make the parts for the models, use the measurements given in the diagrams in the book to draw outlines on construction paper or cardboard. Cut out the parts with extreme care. The accuracy with which you make the parts is an important factor in how well your finished model looks.

Be sure to check whether diagrams have been drawn to scale. If not, use only the measurements given on the diagrams to draw the parts for your model.

3. All of the antique car models require rigid cardboard. It is used mainly for the chassis, bulkheads, and wheels. The cardboard must be rigid enough to hold its shape. As mentioned in the previous chapter, cigar boxes and matting board are excellent for this purpose. Cutting these stiff materials requires more pressure on your knife than cutting thinner paper. To do this, run the knife several times over the drawn line, going deeper with each cut. Then bend the cardboard along the cut line. To make the final cut, either turn the cardboard upright and slice through the portion still holding the sections together, or leave the cardboard flat on your work surface and run your knife repeatedly along the cut line until the pieces separate. If you choose the second method, make sure your work surface is well protected.

All the models are built on a chassis of rigid cardboard. If your cardboard does not have too much printing or design on it, leave it as is. Otherwise, paint out the printing or design with poster paint. In most cases, you need only paint the underside of the chassis; the top side will be hidden by the body of the car.

To make cardboard wheels, use your compass to draw a circle with the diameter given in the diagram. Go over the circle several times with your compass pencil, pressing firmly each time to make a deeply indented circle. This forms a track for your scissors to follow. Draw or paint the wheel design before cutting out the circle. Hold the cardboard to your work surface with small pieces of masking tape while you draw. Be careful to keep the tape clear of the wheel pattern. Then cut the circle with your scissors, turning the cardboard continuously into the blades. This lessens the chances of cutting straight lines instead of curves around the rim of the wheel.

4. Some of the antique car models have one or more curved parts.

14

A few parts bend more than once. Here are two ideas that will help you form these curves:

• Before gluing the part in position, pull it over the edge of your work surface or ruler. Pull gently but firmly with one hand as you press the paper against the table or ruler edge with the other hand. This gives the part a permanent curved shape. By curving the paper in this way, you will make it much easier to glue the part in position, instead of trying to hold it in a curve with glue.

• For parts with more than one curve—curving in one direction, then another—moisten the cut-out part with water. Use a damp cloth or sponge; do not soak the paper. Too much water will make it tear easily. While the paper is moist, you can mold it into any shape you need, however complicated. You may glue the moistened part immediately; it does not have to dry first.

5. Small lengths of drinking straw are needed for some of the parts on the antique car models. When cutting these lengths, insert a pencil or other round piece of wood inside the straw. This serves as a support as you cut around the outside of the straw with your knife. Otherwise, the straw will be crushed by the pressure of the knife.

6. Different lengths of matchstick wood are needed for steering posts, axles, and other small parts. For these pieces, measure the length given in the diagram on a piece of large matchstick wood. Mark the measurement with a pencil. If you are strong enough, you can cut the wood simply by pressing down hard at the marked point with your knife. Make sure the matchstick is resting on a block of scrap wood when you do this.

If the matchstick wood is too tough for this method, place the cutting edge of the knife on the pencil mark and tap the back of the knife gently but firmly with a hammer.

There may be moments as you build these antique car models when everything seems to be going wrong. You may have a streak of cutting parts too small or gluing them on crooked, and wish you were having fun doing something else! But don't give up. Making car models can give you a lot of satisfaction, especially when you succeed in solving difficult construction problems. You can't help having a great feeling of accomplishment when you show off your good-looking finished models.

Finally, remember that all these suggestions, along with others in the pages ahead, are just that—suggestions. All model-makers develop their own ways of doing things. You can draw, cut, and glue by whatever methods you find easiest and most comfortable. Above all, do not hesitate to experiment. Make whatever variations you think will turn your antique car into a better-looking finished model without compromising its historical accuracy. May all your completed antique car models be first-prize winners!

Curved Dash Olds: 1902

Ransom Eli Olds was among the pioneering leaders in the early development of the American auto industry. In the mid-1880s, Ransom joined his father in operating a machine shop in Lansing, Michigan. Shortly afterward, the company began manufacturing gasoline engines. The newly-created automobile was just beginning to catch the public's interest. Since the gasoline engine was one of three types of power units used in the motor car, the father-and-son team felt their product had a bright future.

A restless young man, Ransom was always experimenting in the field of mechanics. So it was natural for him to decide to build automobiles of his own design. Oddly enough, Ransom tried steam and even electricity in his early motor car designs before choosing the gasoline engine as the best form of power. He organized his first automobile building company in 1897, but it quickly failed financially. Undaunted, Ransom established another, the Olds Motor Works, in 1899, and began production in a three-story factory in Detroit. Once again, misfortune struck when fire completely destroyed the plant in March, 1901.

But Ransom Olds was a stubborn young man who refused to admit failure. He took what was left of his company to Lansing and started to build cars for the third time. Luckily, a single model from the Detroit factory had been saved from the fire, the Curved Dash Olds. Ransom had great faith in this car, and was determined to succeed or fail with it.

His persistence paid off. The Curved Dash Olds became a spectacular seller within a few months of its public appearance. To meet the flood of orders for his graceful, dependable little car, Ransom introduced mass-production techniques into his factory. It was the first time such manufacturing methods were employed in the auto industry. Another giant of the early years of the motor car, Henry Ford, was to adapt mass-production methods for building his automobiles with even more sensational results.

The mass-production techniques that Ransom pioneered enabled his factory to turn out more than 2,000 vehicles by the end of 1902. Annual production increased to 5,000 cars by 1904 as demand for the Curved Dash Olds grew. Mass production of the little car helped to keep the price low, about $600, a factor that greatly appealed to the buying public.

The Curved Dash Olds was a lightweight but rugged little motor car. The curved dashboard gave the car a distinctive appearance as well as its name. The car was economical to operate and remarkably trouble-free. It was propelled by a single-cylinder 5-horsepower gasoline engine that gave it a top speed of 20 miles per hour. The driver steered by means of a lever rather than a wheel. Moving the lever to the right or left turned the car in those directions.

The front seat had room for the driver and a passenger, and was protected by a roof. The two back seat passengers, on the other hand, faced rearward and sat outside the roof hoping for fine weather.

Because of a company policy dispute, Ransom Olds left the concern he had founded in 1904. He started a new company called REO, his initials. Ransom was successful once more, and Reo cars were popular with the motoring public until the mid-1930s. Although production of Reo cars ended at that time, Reo trucks continued to be manufactured as part of the production of the White Motor Company.

The Oldsmobile name and car still exist today. The company Ransom organized which produced the curved Dash Olds was absorbed by General Motors Corporation in 1909. The Oldsmobile has been made ever since by this giant automotive manufacturer and is today one of their popular sellers.

BUILDING THE CURVED DASH OLDS OF 1902

Chassis (Diagram 1)
Draw the chassis as shown in Diagram 1 on rigid cardboard, and carefully cut it out.

Body (Diagram 2)
The body of the Curved Dash Olds is made in one piece from construction paper. I chose black for mine, but you may select any color you wish. Draw and cut out the body as shown in Diagram 2. Score and bend along the dotted lines carefully. This will make the four sides fit together evenly and will add to the attractiveness of the finished body.

19

DIAGRAM 1
Chassis

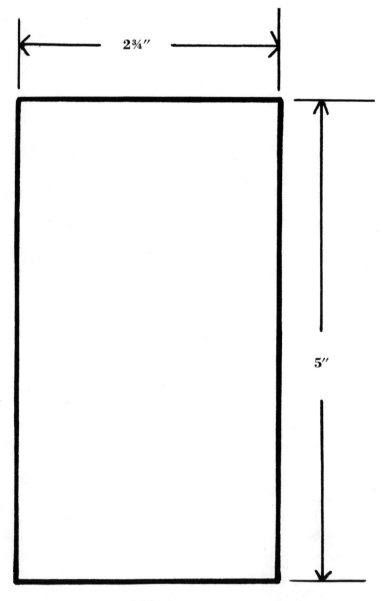

2¾″

5″

Make 1.

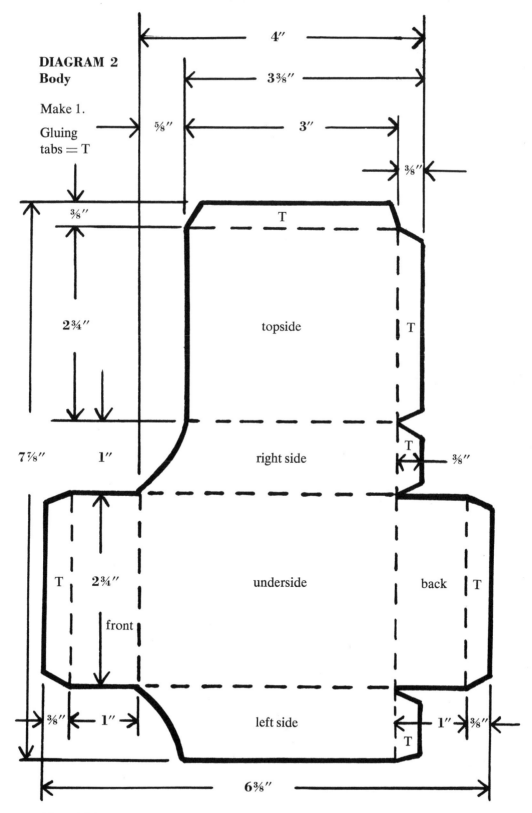

DIAGRAM 2
Body

Make 1.

Gluing
tabs = T

4″

3⅜″

⅝″   3″

⅜″

T

⅜″

2¾″

topside

T

7⅞″   1″   right side

T

⅜″

T   2¾″   underside   back   T

front

⅜″   1″   left side   1″ ⅜″

T

6⅜″

Note: This diagram is not to scale.
Draw and cut out the chassis according to the measurements given.

After the body has been cut and folded, glue the tabs together to form the boxlike body shape. Attach this to the topside of the chassis so that the curved end of the body faces forward and the back end of the body is even with the back end of the chassis.

Front Seat Sides (Diagram 3)
The right and left sides of the front seat are made from bright-colored construction paper. Choose any color you wish, but be sure it contrasts well with the body. Carefully draw and cut out

DIAGRAM 3
Front Seat

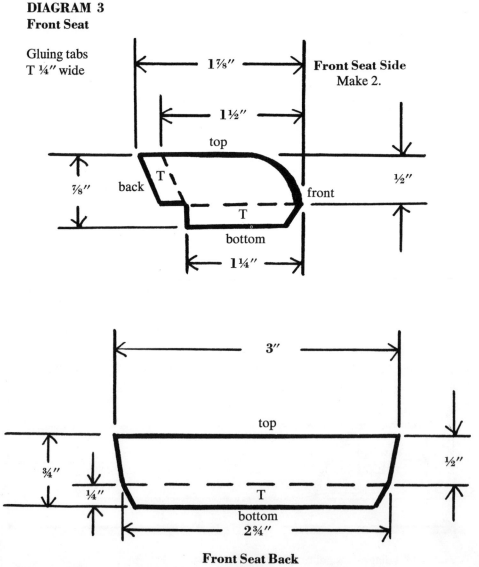

Front Seat Back
Make 1.

the two sides as shown in Diagram 3. Bend the gluing tabs inward so the curved edge of each side will face forward.

Glue the bottom tabs to the top of the body with the rounded ends even with the front edge of the body and with the fold edges even with the body sides.

Front Seat Back (Diagram 3)

The back of the front seat is made from the same color construction paper you used for the sides. Draw and cut it out carefully as shown in Diagram 3. With the long gluing tab bent inward, glue the seat back to the gluing tabs on the back of the front seat sides. Then fasten the long gluing tab to the body of the model. Make sure that the corners where the back and sides meet are straight and tight.

Seat Cushions (Diagram 4)

The seat cushions for the front and back seats are made from a different color construction paper than the sides and back of the front seat. A light green or blue might be good. Draw and cut out the cushions as shown in Diagram 4. Draw the cushion design with pen and black ink or a pointed black crayon. Fold along the dotted lines, making the creased edges as straight as possible. Glue the back seat cushion together at the four corner gluing tabs.

Now the cushions are ready to be attached to the front and back seats. If you measured, cut, and folded accurately, the front seat cushion should fit neatly within the sides and back of the front seat. Glue in place. Be sure the decorated front edge of the cushion is even with the front top edge of the body.

Glue the back seat cushion to the top back end of the body. The cushion should overhang the back edge of the body by approximately ¼ inch.

Back Cushion of Front Seat (Diagram 5)

The back cushion for the front seat is made from the same color construction paper as the seat cushions. Carefully draw and cut

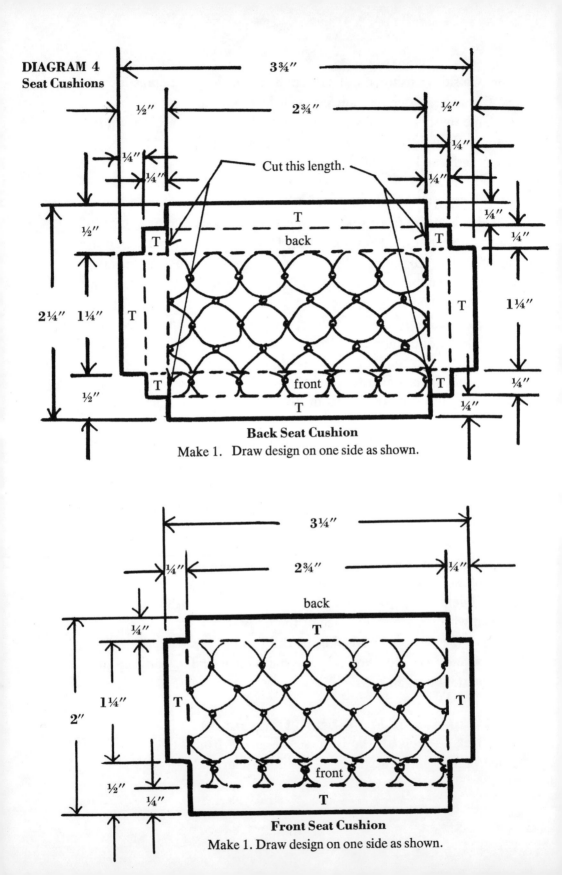

DIAGRAM 4
Seat Cushions

3¾"

½"   2¾"   ½"

¼"

¼"
Cut this length.
¼"

T

T   back   T

¼"

¼"

½"

T

T

T   T

2¼"   1¼"   1¼"

½"

T   front   T

T

¼"

¼"

Back Seat Cushion
Make 1. Draw design on one side as shown.

3¼"

¼"   2¾"   ¼"

back

¼"

T

1¼"

T   T

2"

½"

front

¼"

T

Front Seat Cushion
Make 1. Draw design on one side as shown.

DIAGRAM 5
Back Cushion of Front Seat

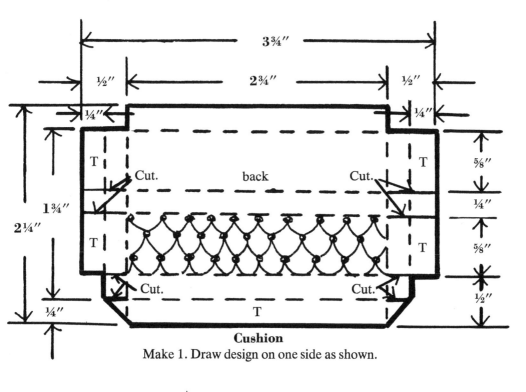

Cushion
Make 1. Draw design on one side as shown.

Support
Make 2.

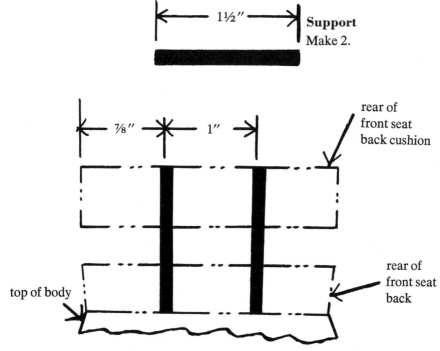

Back Cushion-Support Assembly

out the back cushion as shown in Diagram 5. Draw the cushion design, using pen and black ink or black crayon. Notice that the cushion design is drawn in one panel only. This will be the side facing forward. Fold along the dotted lines, and glue the cushion together at the gluing tabs. Set aside until you have made the two supports.

Back Cushion Supports (Diagram 5)

The back cushion is attached to the front seat by two supports. Cut the supports from large matchstick wood to the length shown in Diagram 5. Paint the supports with black poster paint or drawing ink. Glue the supports to the rear side of the back cushion and front seat, attaching the ends to the top of the body. See Assembly Diagram 5 and the photograph of the finished model on page 49.

Body Panels (Diagram 6)

Two small body panels are attached to the floor just forward of the front seat. They form a low extension of the main body. Draw and cut out the panels as shown in Diagram 6, using the same color construction paper you used for the main body. Fold along the dotted lines carefully, bending the gluing tabs in opposite directions for the right and left sides. Place the panels in position with the square panel ends on the inner side of the curved body ends, and with the front edge of the gluing tabs even with the edge of the chassis. Try to keep the narrow, upright part of the panels as perpendicular to the floor as possible. Glue the panels in place.

Decorations (Diagram 6)

Bright-colored decorations are placed on the right and left sides of the body of the Curved Dash Olds. Draw and cut them from red or orange construction paper, following Diagram 6. Cut the ⅛-inch disc in the center of the oval decoration from white construction paper. Glue the decorations to the sides of the body directly beneath the sides of the front seat. See the photograph of the finished model on page 17 for placement.

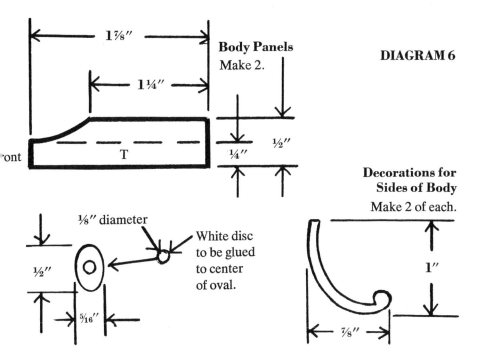

DIAGRAM 6

1⅞"

1¼"

Body Panels
Make 2.

Front

T

½"

¼"

⅛" diameter

White disc
to be glued
to center
of oval.

½"

⁵⁄₁₆"

Decorations for
Sides of Body
Make 2 of each.

1"

⅞"

Back Seat Handrails (Diagram 7)

The Curved Dash Olds had handrails on both the back and front seats. These gave passengers something to hold on to for dear life when rides became too bumpy! Making the rails is a good deal easier than it appears. The hardest task, perhaps, is holding them in place until the glue hardens.

Cut two pieces of thin, paper-covered wire, each about 4¾ inches long. Bend each piece as shown in Diagram 7. Wrap the wire around a pencil or pen to help form the small, sharp bends.

Glue the back seat handrails to the outer sides of the back seat cushion. Be sure to keep the rails as upright as possible until the glue hardens.

The two armrests on the back seat rails are made from ½-inch lengths of large matchstick wood. Cut these as shown in Diagram 7, and paint them with black poster paint. The armrests may be glued in place either before or after the rails have been attached to the back seat. When gluing the armrests to the rails, let the glue dry a bit and become tacky before bringing the two pieces together.

Front Seat Handrails (Diagram 7)

The front seat rails are made from a single piece of paper-covered wire, about 7 inches long. These are a bit more difficult to form because of the length of the wire and the additional curves. But if you use thin wire that is easy to bend, you should not have too much trouble. Follow the pattern for the front seat handrails as shown in Diagram 7, and, again, use a pencil or similar piece of round wood to help shape the bends in the wire.

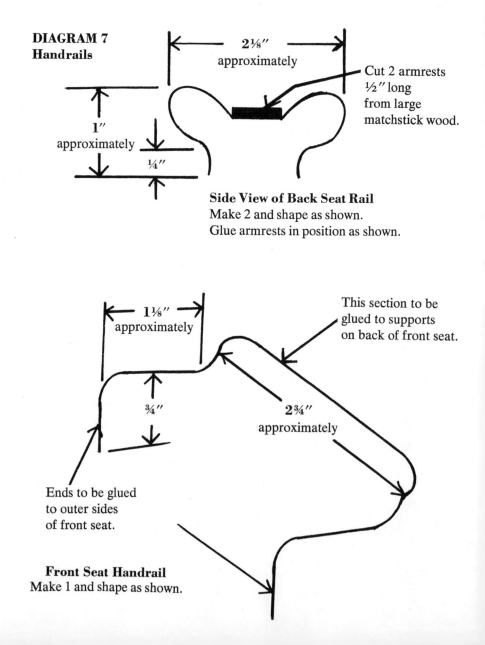

DIAGRAM 7
Handrails

2⅛″
approximately

Cut 2 armrests
½″ long
from large
matchstick wood.

1″
approximately

¼″

Side View of Back Seat Rail
Make 2 and shape as shown.
Glue armrests in position as shown.

1⅛″
approximately

This section to be
glued to supports
on back of front seat.

¾″

2¾″
approximately

Ends to be glued
to outer sides
of front seat.

Front Seat Handrail
Make 1 and shape as shown.

The front seat rails are glued to the back and outer sides of the front seat. Glue the two straight ends of the wire to the outer sides of the front seat and the long straight center to the two supports on the rear of the back cushion. See the photograph of the finished model on page 49 for help with this positioning. Before the glue hardens, make certain that the handrails on the right and left sides of the seat are even with one another.

Curved Dashboard (Diagram 8)

Draw and cut out the curved dashboard as shown in Diagram 8. Use the same color construction paper you used for the body.

Pull the dashboard over the edge of your work surface several times, working from one short side to the other. This will bend the paper and make it easier to shape. Now roll the piece into a cylinder. Wrap a rubber band around the cylinder and leave it for about half an hour. This will give the paper a strong, permanent curve.

Since the dashboard is curved at only one end, flatten about 2⅛ inches of one of the curved ends of the cylinder. Adjust the other curved end so it is approximately 1⅛ inches high. See the side view in Diagram 8.

Glue the curved dashboard to the front end of the chassis. The curved portion should extend beyond the front edge of the chassis, with an overhang of not more than ½ inch. The flattened part of the dashboard forms the floor of the driver's compartment.

Floor Mat (Diagram 8)

The floor mat is made from bright-colored construction paper. I used red but you may choose any color you wish. Draw and cut it out as shown in Diagram 8. Glue it to the floor of the driver's compartment. The back end should fit snugly against the bottom edge of the driver's seat. The forward end should bend part way up the inner side of the curved dashboard. This is the easiest part to install on the entire model!

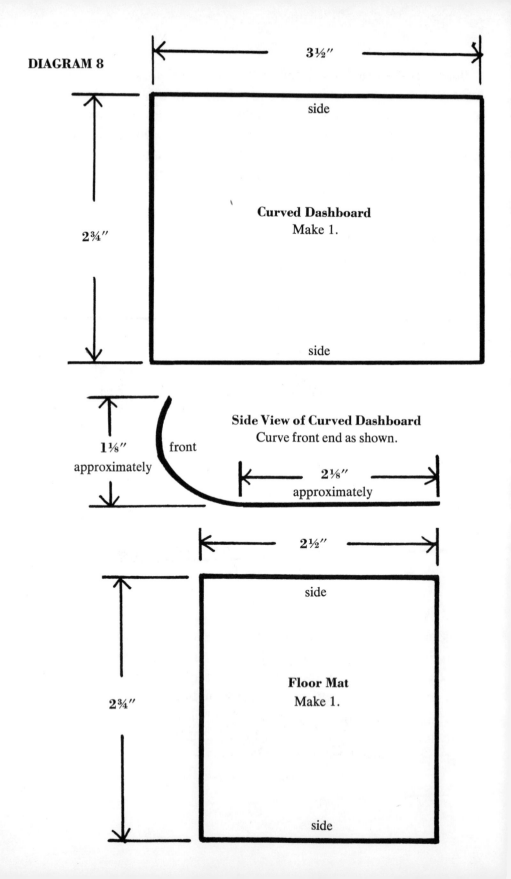

DIAGRAM 8

3½″

side

Curved Dashboard
Make 1.

2¾″

side

Side View of Curved Dashboard
Curve front end as shown.

1⅛″
approximately

front

2⅛″
approximately

2½″

side

Floor Mat
Make 1.

2¾″

side

Steering Lever (Diagram 9)

The steering lever of the Curved Dash Olds consists of three parts: the steering post, the steering handle, and the steering base.

Cut the steering post from large matchstick wood to the length shown in Diagram 9. Paint it with yellow poster paint.

Cut the steering handle from large matchstick wood, too, as shown in Diagram 9. Paint it with black poster paint.

The steering base is made from a piece of rigid cardboard.

DIAGRAM 9
Steering Lever

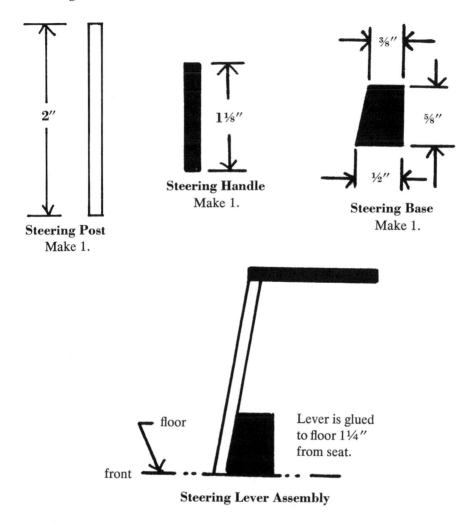

2″

Steering Post
Make 1.

1⅛″

Steering Handle
Make 1.

⅜″

⅝″

½″

Steering Base
Make 1.

floor

front

Lever is glued
to floor 1¼″
from seat.

Steering Lever Assembly

Draw and cut out this piece as shown in Diagram 9. Paint it with black poster paint or ink.

To assemble the steering lever, place the ends of the post and handle together on a flat surface as shown in Assembly Diagram 9. Put a generous amount of glue on the connecting ends. After the two pieces are firmly attached, glue the post to one slanted side of the base. Again, do this with the pieces lying on a flat surface.

When all three pieces are firmly glued, attach the lever to the floor of the driver's compartment. Glue it to the floor 1¼ inches from the front seat and the same distance from the right and left sides of the chassis. See the photograph of the finished model on page 44. Be sure to hold the steering lever straight until the glue hardens. Do not let it tilt to either side.

Rear Footrest (Diagram 10)

As in many of the early automobiles, passengers in the back of the Curved Dash Olds faced rearward. A footrest was provided so their legs did not dangle uncomfortably over the back edge of the car.

The footrest on this Olds model is made from rigid cardboard. Draw and cut it out as shown in Diagram 10. Score lightly along the dotted lines. Score just enough so the sections of the footrest bend easily into position but do not flop loosely.

Paint the footrest with yellow poster paint except for one section, as shown in Diagram 10. This is the foot plate against which passengers would put their feet. Paint this section with black poster paint or cover it with black construction paper.

Bend the footrest into shape shown in Assembly Diagram 10. Attach the footrest to the rear of the body so the edge of the narrow panel is glued snugly against the underside of the overhanging rear cushion. See the photograph of the finished model on page 49.

A support is needed to help hold the footrest to the body of the car. Make the support from rigid cardboard, following the pattern in Diagram 10. Paint it with yellow poster paint. Glue the support under the footrest with one edge attached to the body of the car and the other to the underside of the footrest. See Assembly Diagram 10.

DIAGRAM 10
Rear Footrest

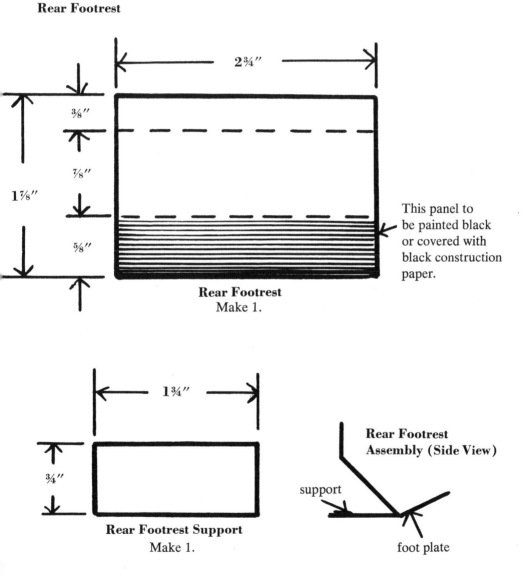

2¾″

⅜″

⅞″

1⅞″

⅝″

This panel to be painted black or covered with black construction paper.

Rear Footrest
Make 1.

1¾″

¾″

Rear Footrest Support
Make 1.

Rear Footrest Assembly (Side View)

support

foot plate

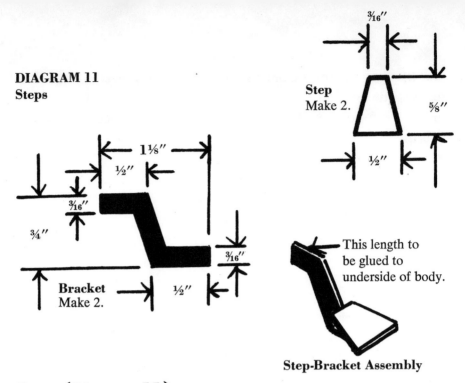

DIAGRAM 11
Steps

1⅛″

½″

³⁄₁₆″

¾″

³⁄₁₆″

Bracket
Make 2.

½″

Step
Make 2.

³⁄₁₆″

⅝″

½″

This length to
be glued to
underside of body.

Step-Bracket Assembly

Steps (Diagram 11)

The Curved Dash Olds had two small steps, one on each side, to help the driver and passenger climb aboard the vehicle. The steps for this model are made from rigid cardboard. Draw and cut them out as shown in Diagram 11. Paint the steps with yellow poster paint.

Each step is attached to the model with a bracket. These, too, are made from rigid cardboard. Draw and cut out the brackets as shown in Diagram 11. Paint both brackets with black poster paint. Glue the steps to the brackets as shown in Assembly Diagram 11.

After the two pieces are firmly attached, glue one step unit to each side of the body on the underside of the chassis. To do this without too much difficulty, turn the car model upside down. Put a generous amount of glue on the edge of the bracket to be attached to the body, as well as on the side of the chassis directly under the forward edge of the front seat. Let the glue in both places dry for a few minutes. Then press the bracket firmly in place. Hold it at a perfect right angle to the chassis until the glue

34

hardens. Leave the model of the car in an upside-down position until both brackets are firmly attached.

Side Frames of Roof (Diagrams 12-13)

Two side frames hold the roof of the Curved Dash Olds model in place. These are made from various lengths of round toothpick wood. In the side frame pattern in Diagram 12, each piece is marked with a number. See Diagram 13 for the length of each numbered piece. Numbers 1 and 2 are starred because these pieces are longer than standard-sized toothpicks. Glue two toothpicks together, if necessary, to make these pieces.

To assemble both frames, draw the pattern in Diagram 12 on a piece of shiny-surface cardboard or smooth wood. Label each piece with its proper number. Place each cut length of toothpick on its corresponding number. Put a generous amount of glue on the ends as you proceed. Before the glue hardens, slide the edge of your knife under each glued joint to pry them free of the work surface. Look at each frame edgewise to make sure the toothpicks lie flat. Then set the frames aside until the glue has thoroughly dried.

DIAGRAM 12
Side Frames of Roof

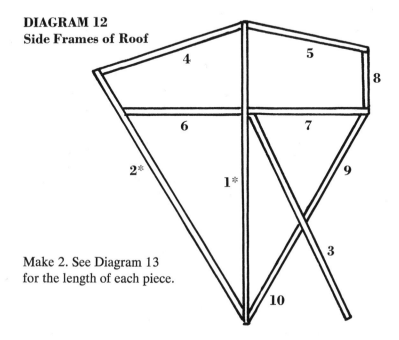

Make 2. See Diagram 13
for the length of each piece.

Roof Crosspieces (Diagrams 13-14)

The side frames are held together by three crosspieces. Cut the crosspieces from large matchstick wood to the length shown in Diagram 13.

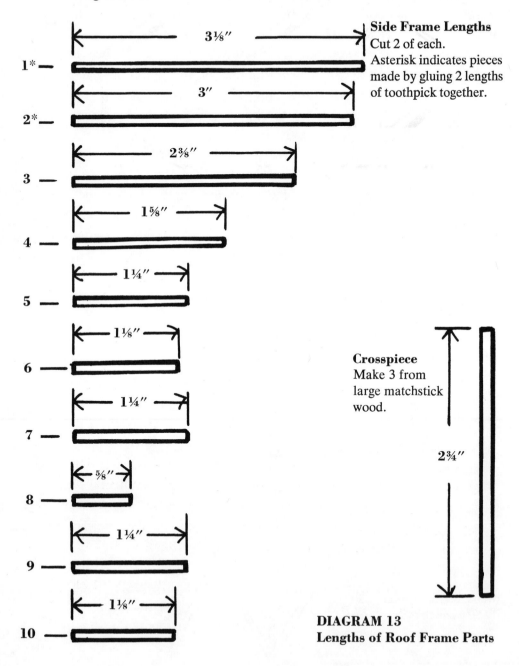

Side Frame Lengths
Cut 2 of each.
Asterisk indicates pieces made by gluing 2 lengths of toothpick together.

Crosspiece
Make 3 from large matchstick wood.

DIAGRAM 13
Lengths of Roof Frame Parts

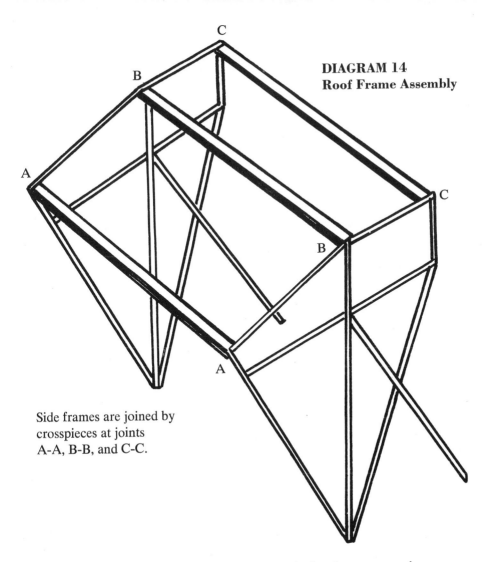

C

B

DIAGRAM 14
Roof Frame Assembly

A

C

B

A

Side frames are joined by
crosspieces at joints
A-A, B-B, and C-C.

Once the side frames are firmly glued, the three crosspieces can be attached. The easiest way to do this is by turning the frames upside down. First glue two crosspieces connecting joints B-B and C-C as shown in Diagram 14. Keep the frames as perpendicular as possible to these crosspieces. Brace a small box, eraser, or similar object against the frames to keep them in position until the glue hardens. After these two crosspieces are firmly attached, glue the last one in place connecting joints A-A.

When the entire frame is assembled and firmly glued, paint the whole unit black. Use poster paint or black drawing ink.

Roof Panels (Diagram 15)

The roof panels of the Curved Dash Olds cover the top and upper sides of the frame. The side roof panels are made and glued in place first.

Draw and cut out these two panels as shown in Diagram 15. Use brown or black construction paper. Glue the tabs of the panels to the framing along side frame parts #4, #5, and #8. Also glue the panels to parts #6 and #7, and the upper sections of #1 and #2. See the photograph of the finished model on page 17.

The top of the roof is glued in place after the side panels are securely attached. Draw and cut out the roof top as shown in Diagram 15. Use the same color construction paper you used for the side panels. Lightly score along the dotted lines. Scoring makes it easier to bend the top into its slanted shape, and to glue it to the frame. Attach the roof top to the frame along both sides, and along the front and back crossbars. The short overhang covers the front crossbar. See the photograph of the finished model on page 17.

The roof frame is now ready to be attached to the car body. Put a generous amount of glue on the outer side of the joints formed by the three upright supports, and on the end of the rear support pieces. Press the sides of the forward joints to the inner sides of the front seat near the curved ends. The ends of the supports should almost touch the top side of the seat cushion. Press the ends of the rear supports to the top edge of the back of the front seat. See the photograph of the finished model on page 17. Make sure the roof is level and does not tilt forward or backward. Hold the supports in place for a few minutes until the glue dries.

The roof of the Curved Dash Olds model is completed with the addition of two back panels that extend downward vertically from the corners of the roof to the rear of the back cushion. Draw and cut out these two panels from the same color construction paper you used for the roof. See Diagram 15. Glue the panels in place, keeping their short top ends even with the top edge of the roof,

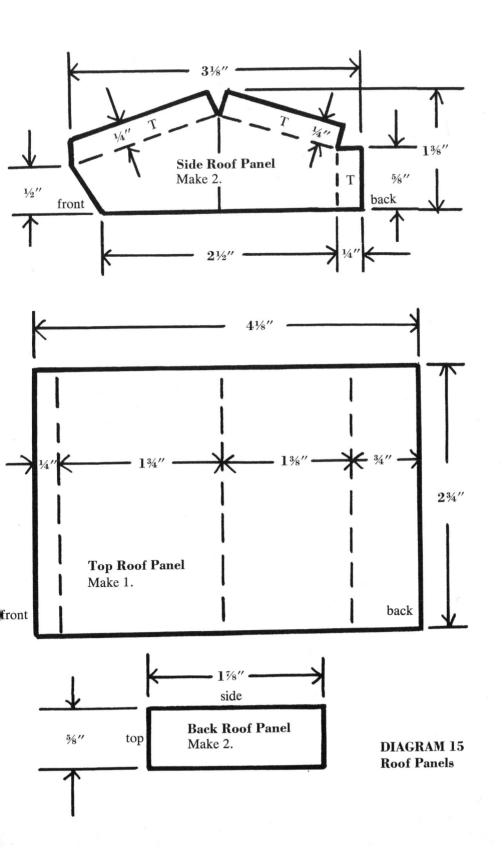

Side Roof Panel
Make 2.

3⅛″

¼″ T

T

¼″

1⅜″

⅝″

½″

front

back

T

2½″

¼″

Top Roof Panel
Make 1.

4⅛″

¼″

1¾″

1⅜″

¾″

2¾″

front

back

Back Roof Panel
Make 2.

1⅞″

side

⅝″

top

**DIAGRAM 15
Roof Panels**

and their long outside edges even with the sides of the top roof panel and back cushion. See the photograph of the finished model on page 49.

**DIAGRAM 16
Wheels**

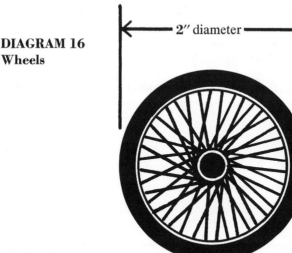

2″ diameter

Make 4.
Draw design as shown
on both sides.

Wheels (Diagram 16)

The four wheels of the Curved Dash Olds are made from rigid cardboard. Draw and cut out the wheels as shown in Diagram 15. Draw the tire and wire spokes design on both sides of each wheel with pen and black ink. Do not forget to paint the edge of the wheels.

Axles (Diagram 17)

Two axles are needed for your Curved Dash Olds model. Cut these from large matchstick wood to the length shown in Diagram 17. Paint the axles with yellow poster paint. Set aside until the spring assembly, axle supports, and wheel boxes have been made.

Spring Assembly (Diagram 17)

The Curved Dash Olds model has a single spring assembly mounted lengthwise on top of the front axle. The spring is made

40

of two halves which are placed one above the other and joined at each end with a small pin.

Draw and cut out the spring pieces from rigid cardboard as shown in Diagram 17. Draw the design on both sides of these pieces with pen and black ink. Cut the ¼-inch pins from the thick portion of a round toothpick and paint them black. Glue one pin to each end of one spring piece. Glue them widthwise so that the length of the pin is the same as the width of the spring. After the pins are firmly attached, glue the second spring piece on top of the pins, sandwich fashion.

The spring assembly has a separator inserted between the spring pieces so that the unit is high in the center and narrow at the ends, much like a real automobile spring. The separator is made from a ¼-inch square of rigid cardboard. Draw and cut out this shape as shown in Diagram 17.

Clamp each end of the spring unit with a hair clip or tie them securely with string. This will prevent the ends from coming apart as the spring pieces are forced away from each other. Put glue on opposite edges of the separator and force the small square between the spring pieces exactly at their center point. This center point is marked approximately by the small circle in the center of the spring design. Set the spring assembly aside until the axle supports have been made and attached.

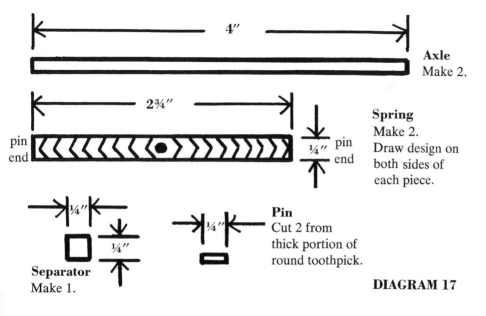

4″

Axle
Make 2.

2¾″

pin end

¼″ pin end

Spring
Make 2.
Draw design on both sides of each piece.

¼″ ¼″

Separator
Make 1.

¼″

Pin
Cut 2 from thick portion of round toothpick.

DIAGRAM 17

DIAGRAM 18
Axle Supports

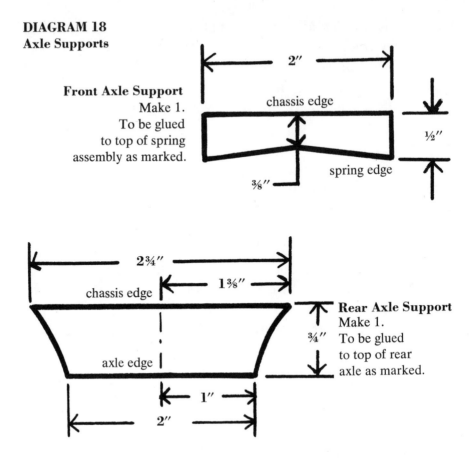

Front Axle Support
Make 1.
To be glued
to top of spring
assembly as marked.

2″

chassis edge

½″

spring edge

⅜″

2¾″

1⅜″

chassis edge

Rear Axle Support
Make 1.
To be glued
to top of rear
axle as marked.

¾″

axle edge

1″

2″

Front Axle Support (Diagram 18)

Draw and cut out the front axle support from rigid cardboard, following Diagram 18. Paint the support black with poster paint or ink. The broad V cut along one edge of the support should match as closely as possible the broad V shape of the outside edge of the spring assembly (to which it is eventually attached). One way to do this is to lay the support flat and trace the V outline of the spring assembly on one long edge.

Attach the support to the front edge of the chassis by turning the car model upside down. Put glue on the straight edge of the support and press it against the underside of the chassis, centering it along the front edge. Be sure to hold the support in an upright

42

position until the glue hardens. See the photograph of the finished model on page 44.

Rear Axle Support (Diagram 18)

The rear axle support for the Curved Dash Olds model is also made from rigid cardboard. Draw and cut it out as shown in Diagram 18. Paint it black with poster paint or ink. Glue this support to the rear edge of the chassis on its underside, following the same procedure you used to attach the front axle support.

Wheel Boxes (Diagram 19)

The Curved Dash Olds model has four wheel boxes made from black construction paper. Draw and cut out these pieces as shown in Diagram 19.

With the tip of your knife, make an "X" cut on each wheel box as shown in Diagram 19. These are openings for the axle ends. Be careful not to make the "X" cuts too large. The axle-wheel box connection should be a snug fit.

Fold along the dotted lines of the wheel boxes carefully. Glue each box together along the gluing tabs. Then glue one assembled box to the center of each wheel with the "X" cut on the outside. This side of the wheel is now the inner or axle side.

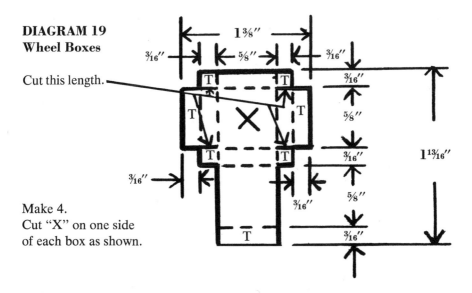

**DIAGRAM 19
Wheel Boxes**

Cut this length.

Make 4.
Cut "X" on one side
of each box as shown.

Wheel-Axle Assembly

The two axles are attached to the wheels at the wheel boxes. Place one of the wheels flat on your work surface. Put a generous amount of glue on one end of an axle and push it through the "X" of the wheel box. Try to keep the axle in a vertical position. If it tilts to one side or the other, your finished model will look as if it is traveling over a bumpy road! One way of checking the angle of the axle is to measure it against another object which you know is straight, such as the edge of a book. Stand this straight edge as close as possible to the axle and wheel, and gauge the axle's position. Repeat this gluing procedure for the other three wheels.

After all four wheels and axles are assembled, they can be attached to the car model. Again, it is best to do this with the car model turned upside down. Glue the back axle first to the bottom

44

edge of the rear axle support, making sure the wheels are the same distance from the sides of the body.

Before attaching the front wheels, glue the spring assembly to the front axle midway between the wheel boxes. See the photograph of the finished model on page 44. After these two units are firmly attached, connect the entire wheel assembly to the front support by gluing the broad V edge of the support to the curved upper surface of the spring. Be sure to keep the wheels the same distance from the sides of the car model and in line with the rear wheels. Once the wheels are in place, the car model is nearly complete. Only the lights need to be made and attached.

Carriage Lamps (Diagrams 20-21)

The Curved Dash Olds model has two carriage lamps which are fastened to the right and left sides of the dashboard. The body of each lamp is made from light green construction paper. Draw and cut out the lamp bodies as shown in Diagram 20. Pull each piece lengthwise over the edge of your work surface to curl the paper and make it easier to roll. Then roll each one into a cylinder ½ inch in diameter and glue it closed. Hold the glued portion in place for a few minutes until it is firmly attached.

The body of each carriage lamp has a top and bottom made from brown construction paper. Draw and cut out the four pieces as shown in Diagram 20. Glue them to the top and bottom of the body pieces.

Each carriage lamp has a top plate, which is glued between two small squares called separators. Draw and cut out the two top plates as shown in Diagram 20, using the same color construction paper you used for the top and bottom pieces. Cut out the four separators from rigid cardboard and paint them with yellow poster paint. See Diagram 20. Glue one separator to the center of the top of each lamp. Glue a top plate on top of each separator, and then glue a second separator to the center of each top plate. See Assembly Diagram 21 and the photograph of the finished model on page 44.

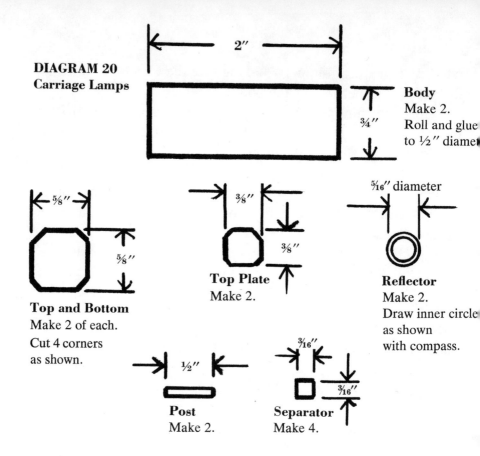

DIAGRAM 20
Carriage Lamps

2″

Body
Make 2.
Roll and glue
to ½″ diamet

¾″

⁵⁄₈″

⁵⁄₈″

Top and Bottom
Make 2 of each.
Cut 4 corners
as shown.

³⁄₈″

³⁄₈″

Top Plate
Make 2.

⁵⁄₁₆″ diameter

Reflector
Make 2.
Draw inner circle
as shown
with compass.

½″

Post
Make 2.

³⁄₁₆″

³⁄₁₆″

Separator
Make 4.

At the front of each carriage lamp is a white reflector. Draw and cut out these pieces from white construction paper as shown in Diagram 20. Cuticle scissors might make it easier to cut these small circles. Draw the inner circle as shown with a compass and pencil, or a special inking compass. Glue one reflector to each lamp body as shown in Assembly Diagram 21 and the photograph of the finished model on page 44.

Each carriage lamp has a short decorative post attached to the bottom. Cut these two pieces from round toothpicks and paint them with yellow poster paint. See Diagram 20. Before gluing the posts in place, turn the lamps upside down. Put a generous amount of glue in the center of each lamp bottom. Let the glue dry for a few minutes until it is tacky. Then press the posts into the glue, holding them in a vertical position until the glue has

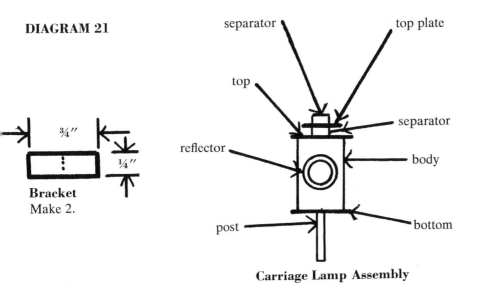

DIAGRAM 21

separator   top plate

top

reflector

separator

body

post

bottom

¾″

¼″

Bracket
Make 2.

Carriage Lamp Assembly

hardened. Set the lamps aside, still upside down, until the posts are firmly attached. In the meantime, work on the brackets for attaching the carriage lamps to the dashboard.

Draw and cut out the two brackets from black construction paper as shown in Diagram 21. Fold each bracket in half along the dotted line to form a right angle. Glue one half of one bracket to the back of each lamp body. Glue the other half to the upper inside edge of the curved dashboard so that the top of each lamp (not the top plate) is even with the top edge of the dashboard. See the photograph of the finished model on page 17.

Headlight (Diagrams 22-23)

In addition to the two carriage lamps, the Curved Dash Olds has a headlight. This is very similar to the carriage lamps except that it is smaller and has no post decoration.

The body of the headlight is made from light green construction paper. Draw and cut it out as shown in Diagram 22. Pull the piece lengthwise over the edge of your work surface. Then roll it into a cylinder with a diameter of ⅜ inch and glue it closed. Hold it closed until the cylinder is firmly attached.

DIAGRAM 22
Headlight

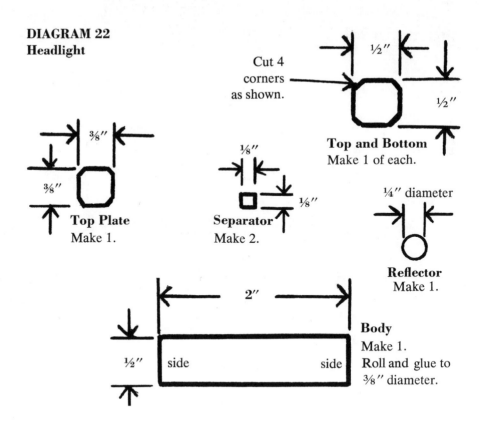

Cut 4
corners
as shown.

½″

½″

Top and Bottom
Make 1 of each.

⅜″

⅜″

Top Plate
Make 1.

⅛″

⅛″

Separator
Make 2.

¼″ diameter

Reflector
Make 1.

2″

½″   side   side

Body
Make 1.
Roll and glue to
⅜″ diameter.

The headlight has a top and bottom made from brown construction paper. Draw and cut out these pieces as shown in Diagram 22. Glue to the top and bottom of the headlight.

The headlight has the same top plate and separator "sandwich" as the carriage lamps. Draw and cut out the top plate as shown in Diagram 22. Use brown construction paper. Draw and cut out the two separators from rigid cardboard as shown in Diagram 22. Paint these small pieces with yellow poster paint. Glue one separator to the center of the headlight top. Glue the top plate on top of this separator. Attach the second separator to the center of the top plate. See Assembly Diagram 23.

A reflector completes the headlight. This is a circle of white construction paper. See Diagram 22 for the size to draw and cut out. Glue the reflector to the front of the headlight body the same

48

distance from both ends. See Assembly Diagram 23 and the photograph of the finished model on page 44. Glue the headlight to the center of the spring assembly and front axle beneath the dashboard. See the photograph of the finished model on page 44.

DIAGRAM 23

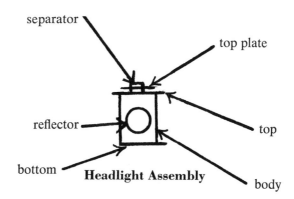

separator

top plate

reflector

top

bottom

Headlight Assembly

body

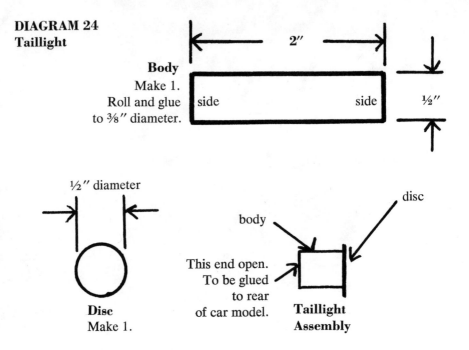

DIAGRAM 24
Taillight

2″

Body
Make 1.
Roll and glue
to ⅜″ diameter.

side   side

½″

½″ diameter

disc

body

This end open.
To be glued
to rear
of car model.

Disc
Make 1.

Taillight
Assembly

Taillight (Diagram 24)

A single taillight completes this model of the Curved Dash Olds of 1902. Draw and cut out the body of the taillight from yellow construction paper as shown in Diagram 24. Pull the piece over the edge of your work surface to curl it. Then roll it into a cylinder ⅜ inch in diameter. One end of the cylinder is covered with a ½-inch disc made from bright red construction paper. Draw and cut out this disc as shown in Diagram 24. Glue to one end of the cylinder. Glue the uncovered end of the cylinder to the lower left corner of the rear axle support. See the photograph of the finished car model on page 49. You are now ready to exhibit your handiwork!

Waverley Stanhope Electric: 1909

The Waverley Stanhope Electric was a quiet, smooth-running motor vehicle. It was typical of the great number of electric cars rolling on the roads of the United States and Europe during the early years of this century. Compared to its chief rival, the gasoline-burning auto, electrics were far more dependable and gave off no unpleasant fumes.

The biggest advantage of electrics, however, was the ease with which they could be started. The driver only needed to flick a switch and the car was underway. By contrast, the driver of a car with a gasoline engine had to turn a crank a number of times before the motor exploded into life. Cranking a car could sometimes be dangerous. If the handle backlashed, it took quick reflexes to get your arm out of the way and prevent a broken hand or wrist. It was mainly because of the difficulty in starting gasoline cars that women preferred to drive electrics.

As one manufacturer of electric cars advertised, anyone could learn to operate an electric in less than half an hour. Steering was controlled by a tiller. There was a hand control for increasing or reducing the vehicle's speed, and a foot pedal for slowing or stopping the car. There was also a small button on the floor which, when pressed, rang a bell to warn pedestrians to get out of the way.

Electric cars looked much the same as their gasoline competitors. Under the motor hood, however, they were worlds apart. For their power, electrics needed a heavy cargo of batteries that weighed a thousand pounds or more. These were stored beneath the body of the car. Electrics also had a complex arrangement of wires running from the batteries to an electric motor, and then on to the vehicle's driving wheels.

While electrics could boast of certain advantages, they also had serious disadvantages, not the least of which was their limited travel range. Depending upon the speed at which they were driven, electric cars could travel a distance of between 50 and 75 miles. Then the batteries usually lost their power and had to be recharged. Owners of electrics always had to know the distance they intended to drive to be sure they had enough power for the return trip.

Despite their weaknesses, electric cars proved quite serviceable and popular. They were particularly numerous in cities, where distances to be traveled were generally short. At the turn of the century, there were scores of electric taxis rolling along the streets of New York City.

The Waverley Stanhope Electric to be made as a model was a

fair-weather car. It offered little protection to the driver or passenger. But all electrics were not like that. Indeed, the majority were enclosed, like today's cars, with soft, overstuffed seats, curtains on the windows and, for an elegant touch, small flower vases at the sides of the windows. These features were obviously intended to appeal to female drivers.

By the late 1920s, electric cars had almost disappeared. Many ended up in automobile museums. Rapid improvements in the gasoline-powered car, particularly the invention of the self-starter, swept the electrics into oblivion.

Today, with so much concern about air pollution and a petroleum shortage, electric cars are staging a comeback. In the United States and Europe, many different types are already being driven and others are in various stages of development. Electric car supporters believe the vehicle is a partial solution to the serious air pollution and transportation problems of many large cities.

BUILDING THE WAVERLEY STANHOPE ELECTRIC OF 1909

Chassis (Diagram 1)
Draw and cut out the chassis as shown in Diagram 1. Use rigid cardboard. Paint the chassis with black poster paint.

Body Sides (Diagram 2)
The body sides of the Waverley Stanhope Electric model are almost all curves, except for the long gluing tabs. These are easier to draw if you use a compass or, even better, if you can borrow a plastic curve used by draftsmen. Draw the two body sides as shown in Diagram 2 on blue construction paper, or any other color you wish. Remember, this will be the main color of your model.

Cut out the two pieces and draw the line design around the edges as shown in Diagram 2. Draw the design on opposite sides

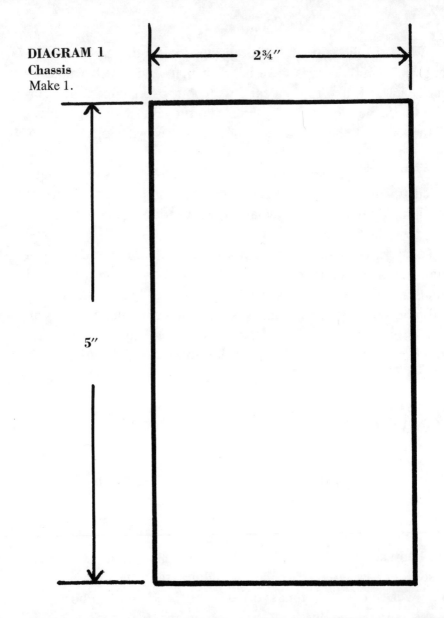

DIAGRAM 1
Chassis
Make 1.

2¾″

5″

of each piece, so the design sides will face outward on your model. Use a pen and black drawing ink, or a crayon that is a good rich black. Glue one body side to the top of each side of the chassis along the long gluing tab, with the front end exactly even with the front edge of the chassis. The extra ⅜ inch at the rear of the chassis will be used for gluing on the trunk.

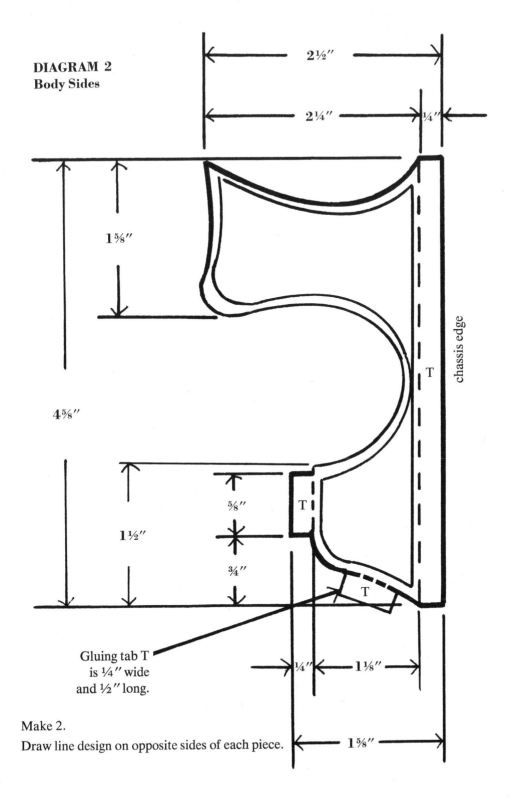

DIAGRAM 2
Body Sides

2½″

2¼″

¼″

1⅝″

4⅝″

chassis edge

T

T

⅝″

1½″

T

¾″

Gluing tab T
is ¼″ wide
and ½″ long.

¼″

1⅛″

Make 2.

Draw line design on opposite sides of each piece.

1⅝″

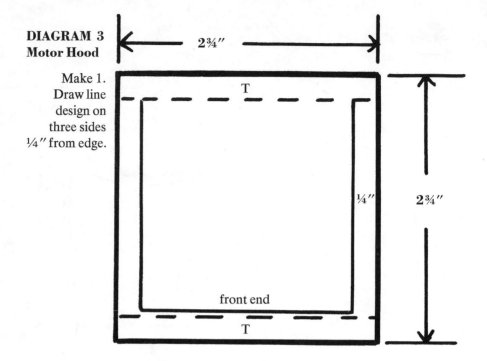

DIAGRAM 3
Motor Hood

Make 1.
Draw line
design on
three sides
¼″ from edge.

2¾″

2¾″

¼″

T

front end

T

Motor Hood (Diagram 3)

The motor hood is a simple square shape. Draw and cut it out from the same color construction paper you used for the body sides. See Diagram 3. Draw the line design along the three sides, ¼ inch from the edge, with pen and black drawing ink.

Before you attach the motor hood, hold the square at the gluing tabs and draw it over the edge of your work surface or ruler to give it a curved shape with the line design on the outside. Fold the gluing tab at the front end along the dotted lines. Glue the tab to the topside of the chassis with the fold edge even with the front end of the chassis. Bend the hood to follow the curve of the front section of the body sides. Glue the hood to the tabs on the body sides with the tabs on the inside of the hood. Be sure the edges of the motor hood are even with the edges of the side panels. See the photograph of the model on page 51. The hood's last gluing tab at the driver's compartment end will be attached to the dashboard later.

56

Body Back (Diagram 4)

Draw and cut out the back of the body from the same color construction paper you used for the sides and hood. See Diagram 4. Like the sides, it has more curves than straight edges. But they are easy to draw, whether you use an instrument or do them freehand.

Fold the gluing tab along the bottom edge and glue to the chassis so it fits evenly between the bottom rear corners of the body sides. Then fold the four curved side gluing tabs, and glue two at a time to the inner surface of the body sides. The back of the body should follow the curve of the rear edge of the body sides.

DIAGRAM 4
Body Back

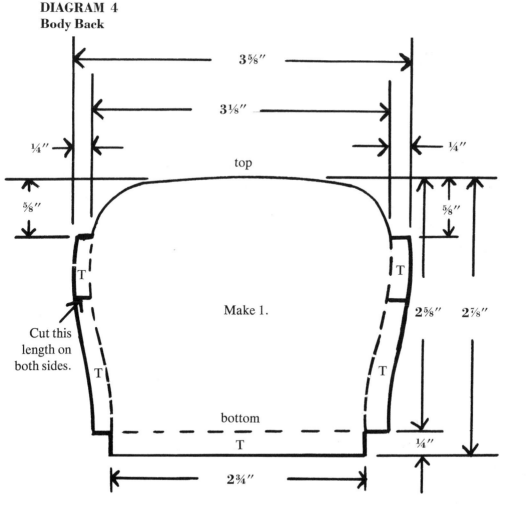

Try to keep the edges of the body sides as even as possible with the back of the body so that gaps between the two pieces do not appear. When the back is firmly attached, the body of the Waverley Stanhope Electric model is complete.

Back Cushion (Diagram 5)

A cushion is attached to the inner side of the back of the body. It is identical in shape to the upper part of the back. Draw and cut

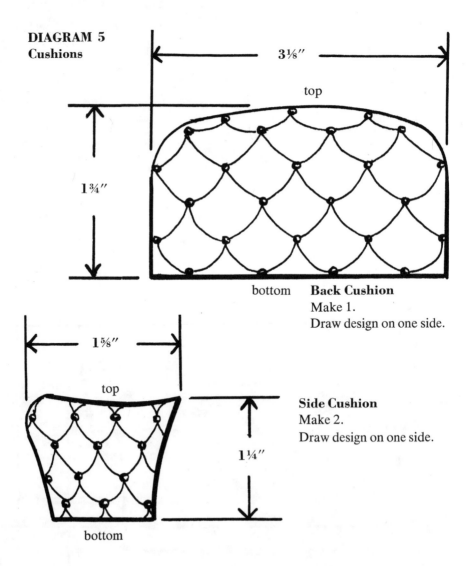

DIAGRAM 5
Cushions

3⅛″

top

1¾″

bottom   **Back Cushion**
Make 1.
Draw design on one side.

1⅝″

top

Side Cushion
Make 2.
Draw design on one side.

1¼″

bottom

out this cushion from yellow construction paper, or any other light-colored paper. See Diagram 5. Draw the cushion design on one side with pen and black drawing ink. Glue the cushion to the inner side of the body back, keeping the top edges of both even with one another. If the cushion extends above the top edge of the back, simply trim it even with your cuticle scissors. See the photograph of the finished model on page 51.

Side Cushions (Diagram 5)

In addition to the back cushion, the driver's compartment has two side cushions. These flat pieces have the same shape as the upper portion of the right and left sides of the body.

Draw and cut out the side cushions, following Diagram 5. Use the same color construction paper you used for the back cushion. Draw the cushion design on one side of each piece with pen and black drawing ink.

Glue the side cushions to the upper portion of the inner surface of the body sides. Again, if the cushion edges extend beyond the edges of the body sides, trim the excess with your cuticle scissors.

Seat Base (Diagram 6)

The driver's seat consists of a seat base and a seat cushion. The seat base forms a boxlike unit with the chassis and the back of the body. Draw and cut out this piece as shown in Diagram 6. Use brown construction paper. Score and fold along the dotted lines.

Place the seat base at the rear of the body between the sides with the seat panel facing upward and the front panel facing forward. Glue the long front panel tab to the chassis floor, the long seat panel tab to the back, and the remaining four tabs to the body sides.

Seat Cushion (Diagram 7)

Draw and cut out the seat cushion as shown in Diagram 7 from the same color construction paper you used for the back and side cushions. Draw the cushion design with pen and black draw-

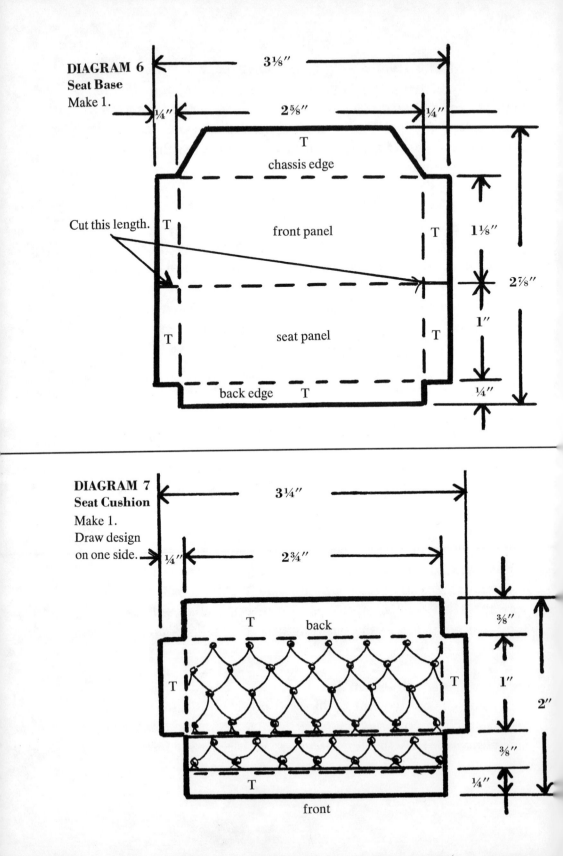

DIAGRAM 6
Seat Base
Make 1.

3⅛″

¼″   2⅝″   ¼″

T

chassis edge

Cut this length.   T   front panel   T   1⅛″

2⅞″

seat panel   1″

T   T

back edge   T   ¼″

DIAGRAM 7
Seat Cushion
Make 1.
Draw design
on one side.

3¼″

¼″   2¾″

⅜″

T   back

T   T   1″   2″

⅜″

T   ¼″

front

ing ink. Carefully score and fold along the dotted lines, bending the tabs and front panel away from the design side.

Glue the seat cushion in place so the narrow patterned panel is even with the front panel of the seat base. Attach the gluing tabs to the top of the seat base, to the right and left sides of the body, and to the back.

Dashboard (Diagram 8)

Draw and cut out the dashboard from black construction paper as shown in Diagram 8. The top edge of the dashboard extends ⅜ inch above the rear of the motor hood. Glue the forward por-

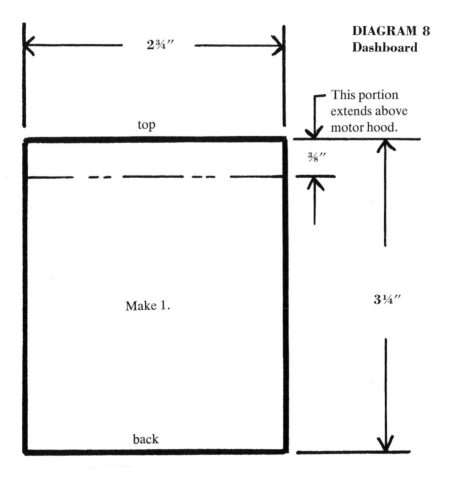

DIAGRAM 8
Dashboard

2¾"

top

This portion extends above motor hood.

⅜"

Make 1.

3¼"

back

tion of the dashboard just below this extension to the remaining gluing tab on the back edge of the motor hood. Position the remainder of the dashboard pattern so that it curves to the chassis floor with its back edge even with the bottom edge of the driver's seat. Glue to the chassis floor. See the photograph of the finished model on page 78.

Trunk Sides (Diagram 9)

Almost all the early cars had a compartment somewhere for carrying tools and spare parts. Breakdowns were frequent and drivers wanted to be prepared. On the Waverley Stanhope Electric, the tool compartment was a separate trunk attached to the chassis behind the body. See the photograph of the finished model on page 78.

Draw and cut out the sides of the trunk as shown in Diagram 9. Use the same color construction paper you used for the body. The curved edge should match as exactly as possible the curve of the lower back of the body. Draw the line design as indicated in Diagram 9, using pen and black drawing ink. Then carefully score and fold along the dotted lines so the design side will face outward.

Trunk Cover (Diagram 9)

Draw and cut out the trunk cover from the same color construction paper you used for the sides. See Diagram 9. Draw the straps as indicated in the diagram, using pen and black drawing ink. Score and fold along the dotted lines with care.

Assemble the trunk by matching the dimensions of the trunk cover panels with the top and back gluing tabs of the trunk sides. Glue one trunk side at a time to the trunk cover. First glue the tab at the back edge of the trunk side to the back panel of the cover. Then glue the tab at the top edge of the trunk side to the top panel of the cover. Be sure the edges of the trunk cover panels are even with the edges of the trunk sides. When the first trunk

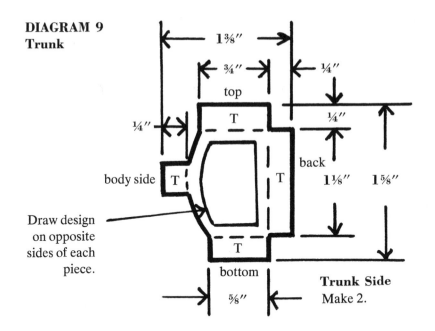

DIAGRAM 9
Trunk

1⅜″

¾″ ¼″

top

T

¼″

¼″

back

body side   T   T   1⅛″   1⅝″

Draw design
on opposite
sides of each
piece.

T

bottom

Trunk Side
Make 2.

⅝″

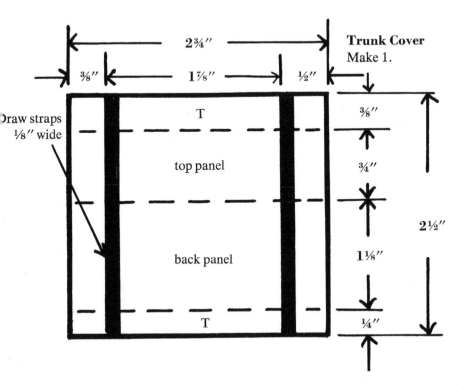

2¾″ **Trunk Cover**
Make 1.

⅜″ 1⅞″ ½″

T

⅜″

Draw straps
⅛″ wide

top panel

¾″

2½″

back panel

1⅛″

T

¼″

side is firmly in place, repeat the gluing procedure for the second side.

Fold under the narrow ¼-inch gluing tab on the trunk cover and glue it to the bottom gluing tabs of the trunk sides. Fold the second trunk cover gluing tab and glue it to the curved edge of the trunk sides. After this tab is secure, place the trunk, curved side inward, on the narrow ledge at the rear of the chassis. Glue the trunk to the back of the curved body along the long tab of the trunk cover and the two small remaining tabs of the sides. Glue the bottom of the trunk to the chassis "shelf." The trunk overhangs the rear end of the chassis by a small amount. See the photograph of the finished model on page 78.

Side Frames of Roof (Diagrams 10-11)

The two side frames of the roof are made from lengths of round toothpick wood attached to a center support of large matchstick wood. Draw the pattern for these frames, as shown in Diagram 10, on a flat piece of wood or stiff shiny cardboard. Label each piece with its number. The length of each numbered piece is shown in Diagram 11. Lengths #2 and #3 are starred because

DIAGRAM 10
Side Frames of Roof

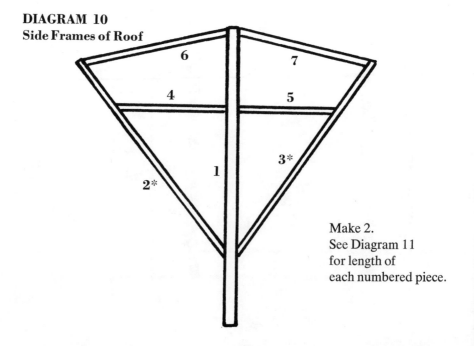

Make 2.
See Diagram 11
for length of
each numbered piece.

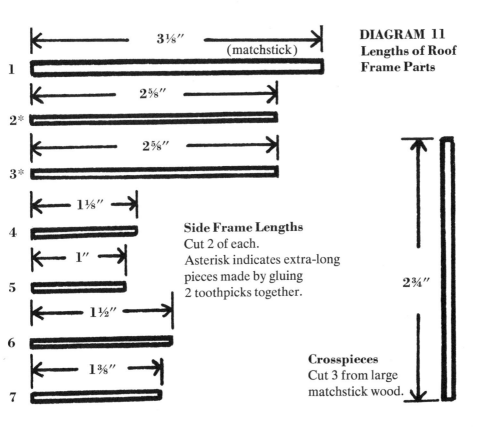

DIAGRAM 11
Lengths of Roof
Frame Parts

1   3⅛″ (matchstick)

2*   2⅝″

3*   2⅝″

4   1⅛″

5   1″

6   1½″

7   1¾″

Side Frame Lengths
Cut 2 of each.
Asterisk indicates extra-long
pieces made by gluing
2 toothpicks together.

2¾″

Crosspieces
Cut 3 from large
matchstick wood.

they are longer than standard-sized toothpicks. To make these pieces, glue two toothpicks together and then cut these to the proper size.

Starting with matchstick length #1, place each cut length of toothpick on the pattern and glue the frames together one at a time. Before the glue hardens permanently, slip your knife very carefully under each of the glued joints to pry them free of the wood or cardboard work surface. Look at the frames edgewise to make sure that all the pieces are straight. Put the frames aside and do not touch them again until all the pieces are securely glued.

Roof Crosspieces (Diagram 11)

The side frames are connected by three crosspieces made from lengths of large matchstick wood. Cut all three pieces to exactly the same length. See Diagram 11.

Roof Frame Assembly (Diagram 12)

The crosspieces join the side frames at joints A-A, B-B, and C-C. See Assembly Diagram 12. Before assembling, turn the side frames upside down. Then glue two crosspieces, connecting joints B-B and C-C. Place supports against the frames, such as a paint bottle or large eraser, to keep them upright until the glue hardens. After these are firmly set, glue the third crosspiece connecting joints A-A, still working in an upside-down position. Since the roof frame is now a single unit, it is easier to attach this last crosspiece. Check to make sure that the roof frame is straight at the top and sides. Then paint the entire frame with black poster paint.

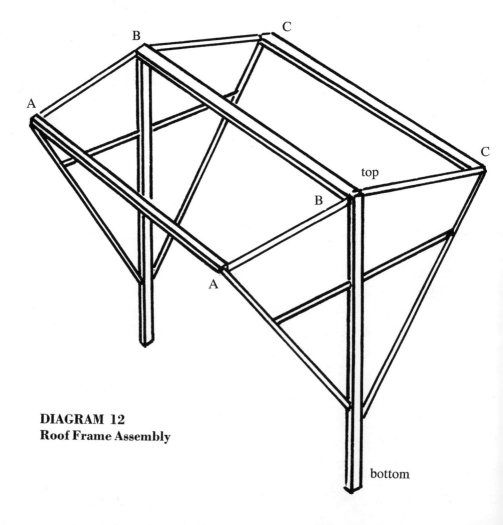

DIAGRAM 12
Roof Frame Assembly

DIAGRAM 13
Side Roof Panels

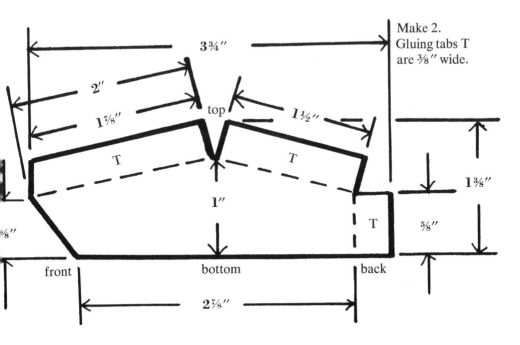

Side Roof Panels (Diagram 13)

The frame is covered with black construction paper along the top, back, and upper portion of the sides. Make and attach the side panels first. Draw and cut out these pieces as shown in Diagram 13. Score and fold the gluing tabs. Be sure to fold the tabs in opposite directions on each panel to adjust for the right and left sides of the roof.

Place the roof panels on the side frames so that the bottom edges of the panels cover and are even with the horizontal bars of the frame. The short tabs should be at the back. See the photograph of the finished model on page 68. Glue the two top gluing tabs of each panel to the top of the side frames. Glue the back tab, center, and front edge of each panel to the side frames along their connecting points.

Top Roof Panel (Diagram 14)

Draw and cut out the roof top as shown in Diagram 14. Use black construction paper. Score lightly along the dotted line. This is the peak of the roof top. From here it slopes gently to the front and to the rear. Glue the roof top to the three crosspieces as well as to the top edge of each side frame.

Back Roof Panel (Diagram 15)

Draw and cut out the roof back as shown in Diagram 15 from black construction paper. Draw and cut out the oval window from white construction paper. Glue it to the roof back ½ inch from the top edge and 1⅛ inches from each side. See Diagram 15.

Glue the tab at the top of the roof back to the rear edge of the roof top, window side facing outward. Before gluing the lower part of the roof back in place, attach the roof unit to the body of

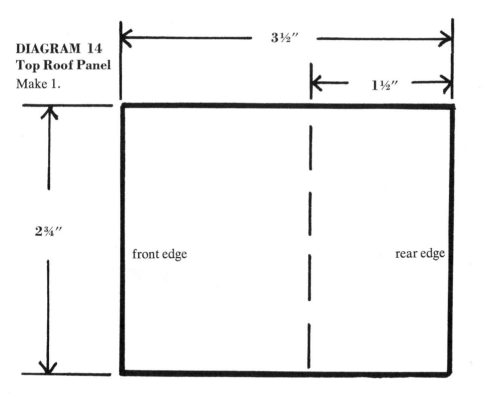

DIAGRAM 14
Top Roof Panel
Make 1.

3½″

1½″

2¾″

front edge   rear edge

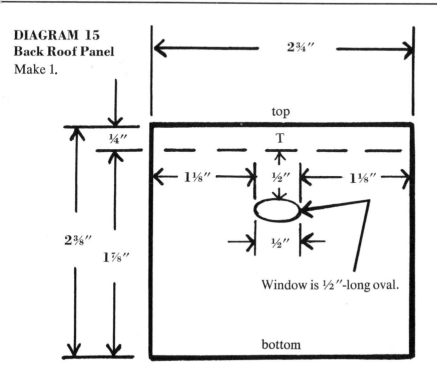

DIAGRAM 15
Back Roof Panel
Make 1.

2¾″

top

¼″

T

1⅛″   ½″   1⅛″

2⅜″

1⅞″

½″

Window is ½″-long oval.

bottom

the model by gluing the lower ends of the side frame supports to the side cushions of the seat. See the photograph of the finished model on page 78. Be sure that the back edge of the roof top is slightly to the rear of the back cushion to allow for the slant of the roof back. Now glue the bottom edge of the roof back to the back of the body. See the photograph of the finished model on page 78.

Mileage Gauge (Diagram 16)
Draw and cut out the mileage gauge as shown in Diagram 16. Use yellow construction paper. This will contrast very well with the black dashboard. Glue the mileage gauge to the dashboard as shown in Diagram 16. Tweezers may make it easier for you to handle this tiny piece.

Speed Gauge (Diagram 16)
The speed gauge is also made from yellow construction paper. Draw and cut it out as shown in Diagram 16. Since this part is even smaller than the mileage gauge, tweezers are a must for handling it. Glue the speed gauge to the dashboard as shown in Diagram 16.

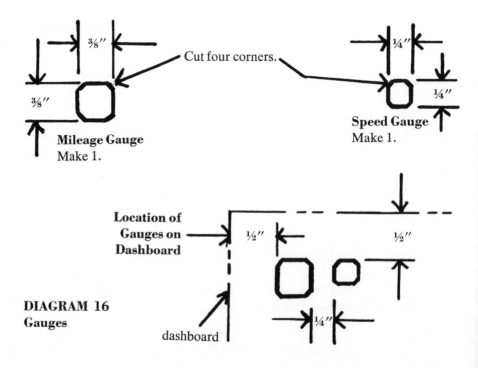

⅜″ ⅜″ Cut four corners.

Mileage Gauge
Make 1.

¼″ ¼″

Speed Gauge
Make 1.

Location of Gauges on Dashboard ½″ ½″

DIAGRAM 16
Gauges

dashboard ¼″

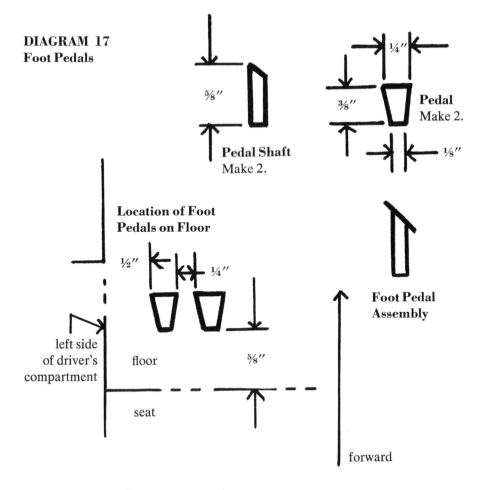

DIAGRAM 17
Foot Pedals

⅝″

Pedal Shaft
Make 2.

¼″

⅜″

⅛″

Pedal
Make 2.

Location of Foot
Pedals on Floor

½″

¼″

Foot Pedal
Assembly

left side
of driver's
compartment

floor

⅝″

seat

forward

Foot Pedals (Diagram 17)

The Waverley Stanhope Electric model has two foot pedals. Each consists of a rigid cardboard pedal and a matchstick shaft.

Draw and cut out the pedals, following Diagram 17. Paint them yellow. Cut the pedal shafts from large matchstick wood so that one end of each piece is slanted. See Diagram 17. Paint the shafts orange.

Glue a pedal to the slanted end of each shaft. Then glue the pedal units to the floor of the driver's compartment as shown in Diagram 17. Let the glue on the bottom ends of the shafts dry for a few minutes before you press them to the floor. The tacky glue will hold the pedals upright until they are firmly attached.

71

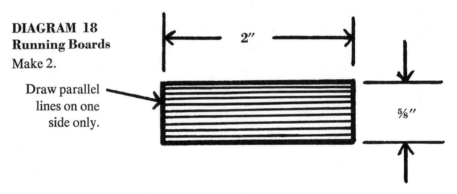

DIAGRAM 18
Running Boards
Make 2.

Draw parallel
lines on one
side only.

2″

⅝″

Running Boards (Diagram 18)
Draw and cut out two running boards from rigid cardboard, following Diagram 18. Draw the parallel lines on one side of each piece, using pen and black ink.

Running Board Brackets (Diagram 19)
Each running board is attached to the car body by two brackets. Draw and cut out the four brackets from rigid cardboard as shown in Diagram 19. Paint the brackets orange.

Glue two brackets to the plain side of each running board as indicated in Diagram 19. When the running boards and brackets are firmly glued, they can be attached to the car body. Turn the car model upside down. Put a generous amount of glue on the ½-inch ends of the brackets. Let the glue dry for a few minutes until it becomes tacky. Then press the bracket ends against the underside of the chassis. Try to center the running boards and brackets directly beneath the curved openings of the driver's compartment. See the photograph of the finished model on page 68. You might have to support the running board units with bottles of paint or other small objects until the glue hardens. Wait until the running boards are firmly attached before turning the car model right side up.

Leaf Spring Units (Diagram 20)
The Waverley Stanhope Electric has four leaf spring units, one beside each wheel. Each unit is made up of two leaf springs, two pins, and one separator.

Draw and cut out eight leaf springs as shown in Diagram 20. Use rigid cardboard. Draw the spring design on both sides of each leaf spring, using pen and black ink.

Two leaf springs are joined together by two small pins, which are glued between them at both ends. Cut the ¼-inch pins from lengths of round toothpick. Paint the eight pins black. Glue the pins between the leaf springs as shown in Assembly Diagram 20.

A separator is also placed between the leaf springs to give the unit its bowed shape. Four separators are needed, one for each spring unit. Draw and cut out these pieces from rigid cardboard as shown in Diagram 20. Paint the separators black.

Before gluing the separators in place, clamp the ends of the leaf springs together with hair clips, or tie them with string. This will prevent the ends from coming apart when the separators are in-

DIAGRAM 19

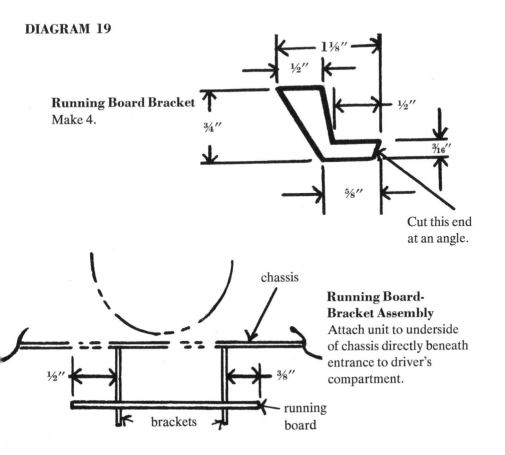

Running Board Bracket
Make 4.

1⅛″
½″
½″
¾″
³⁄₁₆″
⅝″

Cut this end
at an angle.

chassis

**Running Board-
Bracket Assembly**
Attach unit to underside
of chassis directly beneath
entrance to driver's
compartment.

½″
⅜″

brackets

running
board

serted. Put glue on the ¼-inch sides of one separator. Slide it between two leaf springs in the exact center of the spring unit. Twist it upward to a vertical position. Adjust the separator so its sides are even with the sides of the leaf springs. See Assembly Diagram 20. Follow the same procedure for each of the leaf spring units.

After all four leaf spring units are assembled and firmly glued, they are ready to be attached to the underside of the chassis. Turn the car model upside down, and place one spring unit in each corner of the chassis. The separator in each spring unit should be even with the front or rear edge of the chassis so that only half of each unit extends beyond the chassis. Try to keep the long outside edge of each spring unit in line with the right or left side of the chassis. When the spring units are in the right position, glue the center point of the upper leaf spring to the chassis. Check to make sure that the spring units are parallel to one another so that the end of one spring unit does not tilt up while the end of its neighbor tilts down. See the photographs of the finished car model on page 68.

DIAGRAM 20
Leaf Spring Units

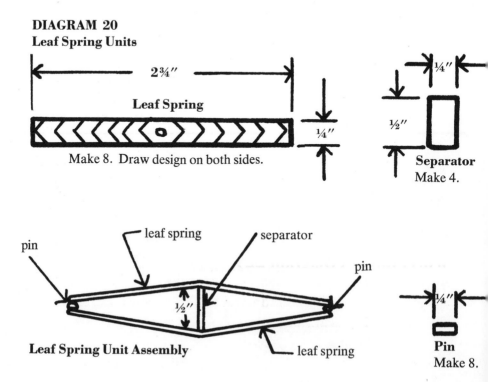

DIAGRAM 21
Wheels

2¼″ diameter

Make 4.
Draw design on both sides.

Wheels (Diagram 21)

The four wheels of the Waverley Stanhope Electric model are made from rigid cardboard. Draw and cut them out as shown in Diagram 21. Draw the wheel design on both sides of each wheel with pen and black ink.

Wheel Boxes (Diagram 22)

In the center of each wheel is a wheel box, which connects the wheel to the axle. Draw and cut out four wheel boxes as shown in Diagram 22, using black construction paper. With the tip of

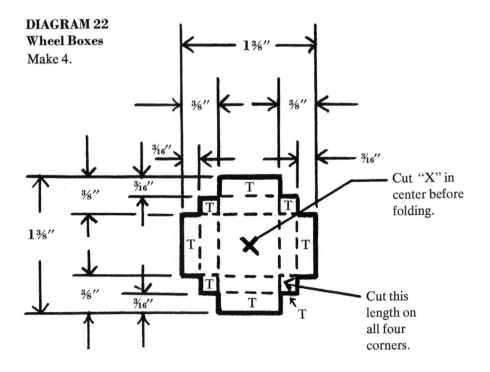

DIAGRAM 22
Wheel Boxes
Make 4.

1⅜"

⅜" ⅜"

³⁄₁₆" ³⁄₁₆"

Cut "X" in center before folding.

³⁄₁₆"

⅜"

1⅜"

⅜"

⅜" ³⁄₁₆"

T T T T T T T T

Cut this length on all four corners.

your knife, cut an "X" opening in the exact center of each piece as shown in Diagram 22. Be careful not to make the "X" openings too large. The ends of the axles are to be inserted in these openings, and if they are too big it will be difficult to make firm wheel-axle attachments.

Fold along the dotted lines carefully. It is important for the wheel boxes to have perfectly straight sides. Otherwise, when the axles and wheels are glued to the boxes, the entire model will be thrown off balance. Glue each box together along the corner gluing tabs.

Glue one wheel box in the center of each wheel. Put a generous amount of glue on each box and make sure the "X" opening faces outward.

Double Axles (Diagram 23)
The Waverley Stanhope Electric model has two identical double

76

axles. Cut each from large matchstick wood. See Diagram 23 for the lengths to cut. Glue the long and short lengths together as shown in Diagram 23. Paint the units with orange poster paint.

Before gluing, insert the axle ends in the "X" openings of the wheel boxes, as shown in Assembly Diagram 23, to find the best combination of snug-fitting pieces. Then attach one axle end at a time to each wheel and wheel box. Put a generous amount of glue on the end of the longer axle length and slide it into the "X" opening at a perfect right angle to the wheel. See Diagram 23. Check to make sure the wheel is not tilted, then repeat for the other three wheels.

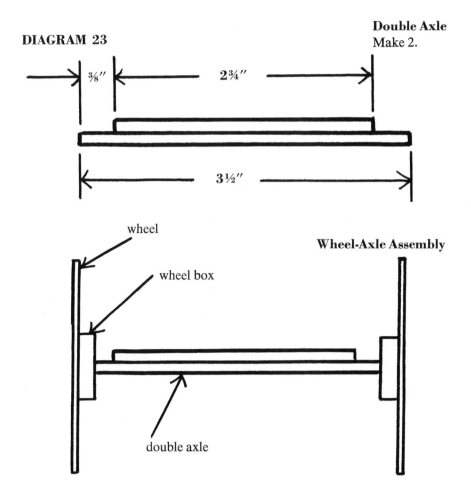

Double Axle
Make 2.

DIAGRAM 23

⅜" 2¾" 3½"

wheel

wheel box

Wheel-Axle Assembly

double axle

Wheel-Axle Attachment

After the wheels, wheel boxes, and axles are firmly assembled, they are attached to the underside of the leaf springs. It is best to do this with the car model in an upside-down position. Glue the ends of the shorter length of a double axle to the centers of the front or rear leaf springs. The ends should be in line with the separators, and the entire axle length should be parallel to the front or rear edge of the chassis. Also try to keep the wheels the same distance away from the right and left sides of the chassis. Repeat for the remaining wheel-axle unit.

Steering Unit (Diagram 24)

The steering unit consists of a steering handle, steering shaft, steering shaft attachment, and steering crossbar.

The steering handle is made from a length of round toothpick.

DIAGRAM 24
Steering Unit

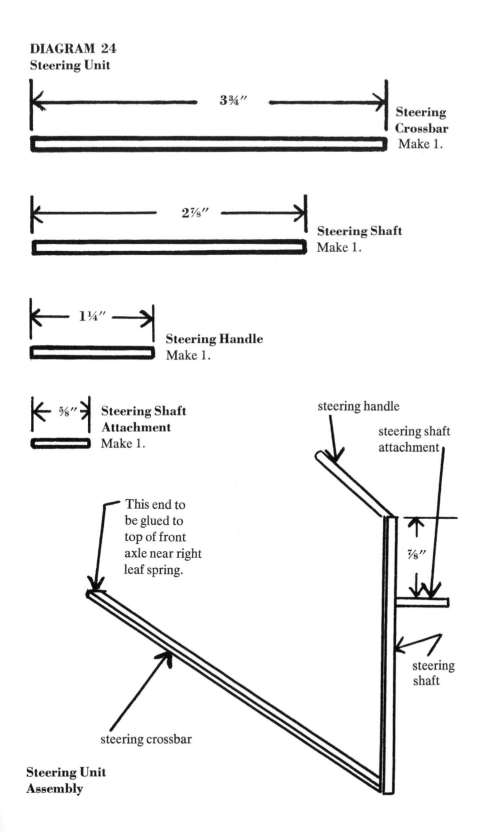

3¾″

**Steering
Crossbar**
Make 1.

2⅞″

Steering Shaft
Make 1.

1¼″

Steering Handle
Make 1.

⅝″ **Steering Shaft
Attachment**
Make 1.

steering handle

steering shaft
attachment

This end to
be glued to
top of front
axle near right
leaf spring.

⅞″

steering
shaft

steering crossbar

**Steering Unit
Assembly**

Cut the toothpick to the length shown in Diagram 24 and paint it with orange poster paint.

The steering shaft is made from a length of large matchstick wood. Cut the matchstick to the length shown in Diagram 24 and paint it with black poster paint.

The steering shaft attachment is a short length of round toothpick. Cut the toothpick as shown in Diagram 24, and paint it orange.

The steering crossbar is made from a length of large matchstick wood. Cut the matchstick to the measurement shown in Diagram 24 and paint it black.

Steering Unit Assembly (Diagram 24)

After all the parts of the steering unit have been cut and painted, they are ready to be assembled as shown in Diagram 24. You will find it easier to attach the pieces if you put lots of glue on the ends to be joined. Allow the glue to dry for a few minutes to become tacky before pressing the ends together.

Glue the steering handle at right angles to one end of the steering shaft. Glue the steering shaft attachment also at right angles to the steering shaft, but pointing in a different direction from the handle. See Diagram 24.

Position and glue the short steering shaft attachment piece to the left side of the body and approximately even with the top edge of the seat cushion. The lower end of the steering shaft should be outside the car body and should extend slightly below the chassis. The steering handle should automatically be inside the driver's compartment at the left side of the seat where the driver would sit. See the photograph on page 51.

After the shaft attachment is firmly in position, place one end of the steering crossbar on the free end of the steering shaft, and the other end on the front axle near the right leaf spring. Glue in place. Hold or clamp the crossbar ends until they are securely attached.

Front Fenders (Diagram 25)

The front and back fenders of the Waverley Stanhope Electric model are both flattened S-shapes, but the front fenders are shorter than those at the back.

Draw and cut out the front fenders as shown in Diagram 25. Use black construction paper. To make the fender curves, first pull one end of each fender lengthwise over the edge of your work surface or ruler several times. Then turn the fender over and curve the opposite end in the same way. Shape the fenders to match the side view in Diagram 25. Bend, but do not score, the back end of the fender to form a sharp right angle. Glue this to the front edge of the underside of the running board. See the photograph of the finished model on page 68.

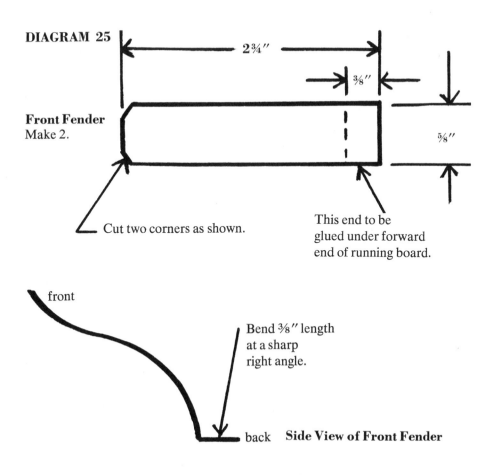

DIAGRAM 25

2¾″

⅜″

Front Fender
Make 2.

⅝″

Cut two corners as shown.

This end to be glued under forward end of running board.

front

Bend ⅜″ length at a sharp right angle.

back   **Side View of Front Fender**

Rear Fenders (Diagram 26)

Draw and cut out the rear fenders from black construction paper as shown in Diagram 26. Curve these pieces in the same way as the front fenders. First pull one end lengthwise over the edge of your work surface several times, and then turn the fender over and curve the other end in the same way. The final fender shape should match the side view in Diagram 26.

Bend, but do not score, the ⅜-inch tab on each fender to form a sharp right angle. Glue these tabs to the rear edge of the underside of each running board. Because of their length, these fenders need extra support to hold them above the wheels. Hold the rear fenders at the same level above the wheels, and glue their inner edges to the sides of the trunk. Hold the glued fenders in place for a few minutes until they are firmly attached. See the photograph of the finished model on page 68.

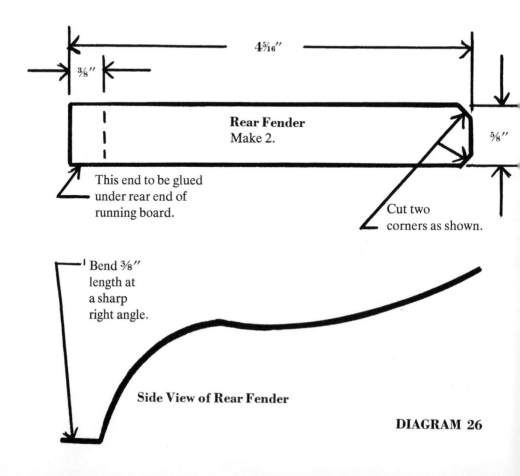

$4\frac{5}{16}''$

$\frac{3}{8}''$

Rear Fender
Make 2.

$\frac{5}{8}''$

This end to be glued
under rear end of
running board.

Cut two
corners as shown.

Bend ⅜''
length at
a sharp
right angle.

Side View of Rear Fender

DIAGRAM 26

Carriage Lamps (Diagram 27)

The Waverley Stanhope Electric model has two carriage lamps, one on each side of the motor hood. The carriage lamp is made up of the carriage lamp body, top and bottom, top plate, knob, and bracket.

The carriage lamp body is made from yellow construction paper. Draw and cut out these two pieces as shown in Diagram 27. Pull each piece lengthwise over the edge of your work surface several times to give it a curved shape. Then roll it into a cylinder $3/8$ inch in diameter. Overlap the $1/2$-inch ends and glue them closed. If one end of the overlap is too long, trim it with your scissors.

The top and bottom parts of the carriage lamps are identical. Draw and cut out these pieces as shown in Diagram 27. Use rigid cardboard and paint each piece black. Glue one piece to each end of the carriage lamp bodies. Be sure the cylinder shape is in the exact center of the end pieces. See Assembly Diagram 27 and the photograph of the finished model on page 68.

The top plates for the carriage lamps are made from rigid cardboard. Draw and cut out the two top plates as shown in Diagram 27 and paint them black. Glue one top plate to the center of the top of each lamp. See Assembly Diagram 27.

The carriage lamp knob is also made from rigid cardboard. Draw and cut out the two knobs as shown in Diagram 27 and paint them orange. Glue one knob in the center of each top plate. See Assembly Diagram 27.

Each carriage lamp is attached to the body of the car model by a bracket made from rigid cardboard. Draw and cut out these pieces as shown in Diagram 27. Paint both brackets orange. Glue one bracket to the bottom of each lamp so that the $1/2$-inch bracket edge forms a right angle with the lamp bottom. See Assembly Diagram 27.

Glue one carriage lamp to each upper side of the motor hood near the dashboard. Glue the lamps along the $1/2$-inch bracket

DIAGRAM 27
Carriage Lamps

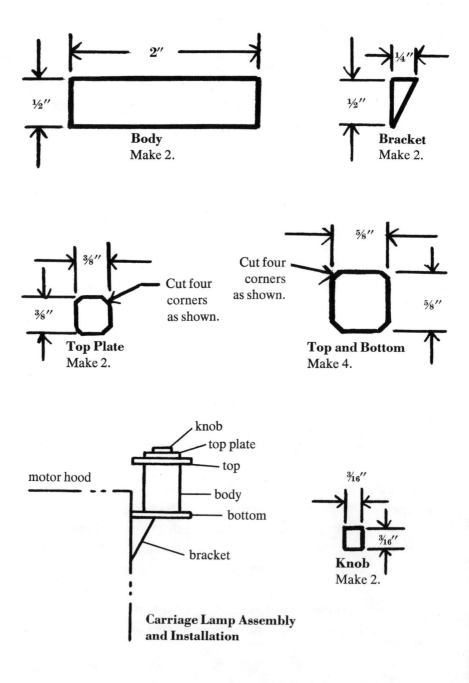

2″

½″

Body
Make 2.

¼″

½″

Bracket
Make 2.

⅜″

⅜″

Cut four corners as shown.

Top Plate
Make 2.

Cut four corners as shown.

⅝″

⅝″

Top and Bottom
Make 4.

knob

top plate

top

motor hood

body

bottom

bracket

**Carriage Lamp Assembly
and Installation**

³⁄₁₆″

³⁄₁₆″

Knob
Make 2.

DIAGRAM 28
Taillight

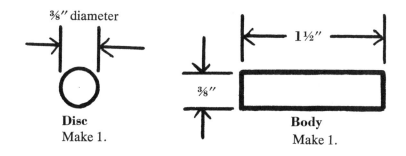

⅜″ diameter

Disc
Make 1.

1½″

⅜″

Body
Make 1.

edge and the lamp bottom edge. See Assembly Diagram 27 and the photograph of the finished model on page 78.

Taillight (Diagram 28)

The Waverley Stanhope Electric has one taillight made up of the taillight body and taillight disc.

The taillight body is made from black construction paper. Draw and cut it out as shown in Diagram 28. Pull the piece lengthwise over the edge of your work surface to form a curved shape. Then roll and glue it into a cylinder ⅜ inch in diameter.

Use bright red construction paper to make the taillight disc. Draw and cut it out as shown in Diagram 28. Glue the disc to one end of the taillight body. Place the finished taillight in the lower left corner of the trunk so that it rests on top of the left rear spring. Glue in place. This completes the model of the Waverly Stanhope Electric of 1909.

Stanley Steamer: 1911

Freeland O. and Francis E. Stanley were identical twin brothers. They looked alike, dressed alike, and carried on their life's work together. Born in 1849, the twins were raised on a farm in Kingfield, Maine. But farming was not for them. As young men they displayed exceptional talent for mechanics. It was in this field that the Stanley twins were destined to make their mark.

The Stanley brothers left their farm home for the more industrialized state of Massachusetts. Here, they felt, were more opportunities for putting their mechanical skills to work. Within a few years they developed and patented several ideas, the most important of which dealt with photography. Their Stanley Dry Plate, which they sold to the Kodak Company, was a highly successful improvement for taking pictures. This, along with other patents almost as rewarding, made the Stanley twins financially comfortable. But their real accomplishments were still to come.

By the late 1890s, the automobile was beginning to appear in a variety of forms and was arousing great curiosity in both the United States and Europe. In 1896, the Stanley brothers visited a fair in Brockton, Massachusetts, where the revolutionary horseless carriage was exhibited. They were fascinated by their first sight of the mechanical wonder and, even before leaving the fairgrounds, had decided to build a car of their own. The twin brothers were confident theirs would be superior to the model on exhibit.

The Stanley twins set up a shop in Newton, Massachusetts, and soon were deeply involved in designing and building their first automobile. Since steam power was the best-known and most highly developed man-made energy source of its day (compared to the still crude gasoline engine and the limited efficiency of electric power), the Stanley brothers chose it for their pioneering motor car. By 1897, they were rolling around the streets of Newton in the first Stanley Steamer. Needless to say, the town's citizens were fascinated by the wondrous machine.

Orders for similar horseless carriages soon arrived in the Stanley shop and almost overnight the brothers had a flourishing business on their hands. In fact, they had so many requests for cars that they were hardpressed to meet the demand. Mass production of motor cars was still in the future, and their autos were entirely handcrafted. Despite slow building methods, the Stanley twins were managing to turn out 100 Steamers a year by 1898.

The Stanley brothers sold their original auto manufacturing business to the Locomobile Company in 1899. But the twins could not resist the fascination of motor cars and started a new company. They designed and built an entirely different type of steam car, one of which is the model you will build.

Stanley Steamers, the earliest models as well as those built later, were outstanding motor cars. They were rugged and fast. Freeland Stanley once demonstrated the toughness of his car by driving it up towering Mt. Washington, 6288 feet high, in New Hampshire. With his wife as a passenger, Freeland puffed his way up the winding, rough road in two hours and ten minutes, the first car ever to make that journey.

If the owner of a Stanley Steamer wanted speed, the car could give it in abundance. Except for cars that were specially prepared for racing, Stanley Steamers under a full head of steam could probably outspeed any other vehicle on the road in the late nineteenth and early twentieth centuries. Curious to know how fast their car could really go, the Stanley twins prepared one for a speed test on Ormond Beach, Florida, in 1906.* Only the body of the car was altered for the test, to make it more streamlined. The steam power unit was the same as the one used in the cars sold to the public.

Fred Marriott, a test driver for the Stanley Company, was at the wheel of the powerful car as it sped over the firm sands of the beach. He flashed through a measured mile course at a sizzling rate of 127.66 miles per hour, a new world's speed record for automobiles. And yet, at the end of his run, Marriott said he still had plenty of reserve power but thought it wiser not to use it.

The following year Marriott was back at Ormond Beach, determined to go all out with the Steamer. At the height of his run, the car hit a soft spot on the beach, causing Marriott to lose control of the vehicle. The car was totally wrecked and Marriott himself was almost killed. Describing the test run later, he said the needle on the speedometer had touched 197 miles per hour when the mishap occurred.

By the mid-1920s the Stanley twins were through with auto-

*See *Car Racing Against The Clock* by Frank Ross, Jr., Lothrop, Lee & Shepard Company, New York: 1976.

mobile manufacturing for good. The few Stanley Steamers existing today are as much sought after by antique car collectors as they were by original buyers decades ago.

BUILDING THE 1911 STANLEY STEAMER

Chassis (Diagram 1)

The chassis for the Stanley Steamer is made from rigid cardboard. Draw and cut it out, using the dimensions given in Diagram 1. Paint the entire chassis with black poster paint.

Motor Bulkheads #1 and #2 (Diagram 2)

Two motor bulkheads serve as vertical supports for the motor compartment of the Stanley Steamer model. Draw and cut out bulkheads #1 and #2 from rigid cardboard as shown in Diagram 2. Cut the angles on the upper corners as carefully as possible.

Make a small hole through bulkhead #2 for the steering post as shown in Diagram 2. Use a sharp-pointed tool to begin the hole, then enlarge it with a pencil point. Make the hole just large enough for a length of large matchstick to slide through.

Glue the two bulkheads to the chassis at perfect right angles, ¼ inch in from each side. The bottom edge of bulkhead #1 is 1 inch from the front end of the chassis. Bulkhead #2 is 2¼ inches from the front end. See Diagram 2. It is easier to attach the motor bulkheads if you let the glue dry for a few minutes and become tacky before you put them in place. The bulkheads might need supports on each side to keep them in a vertical position until they are firmly attached.

Nose Bulkheads #3 and #3A (Diagram 3)

The front end of the motor compartment of the Stanley Steamer is a perfect half circle. Nose bulkheads #3 and #3A provide the supports for this shape. Draw and cut out these pieces as shown in Diagram 3. Use rigid cardboard.

Glue the straight edges of these bulkheads to bulkhead #1 as

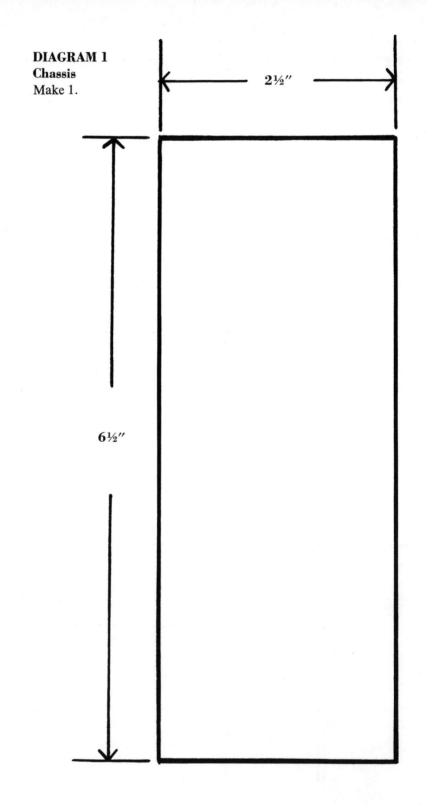

DIAGRAM 1
Chassis
Make 1.

2½″

6½″

shown in Diagram 3. Bulkhead #3A is easy to attach since it rests on the floor of the chassis. Bulkhead #3 is attached 1 inch above bulkhead #3A and ⅜ inch from the top of bulkhead #1. Wait until the glue becomes tacky before putting this bulkhead into position. You might place a support under bulkhead #3 until it is firmly attached. Or you can turn the entire chassis on its front end so the nose bulkheads are at right angles to your work surface and bulkhead #1.

DIAGRAM 2
Motor Bulkheads
#1 and #2

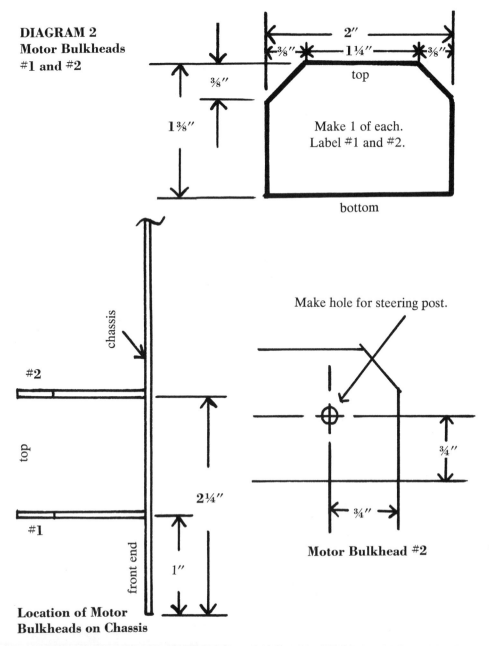

2″

⅜″ 1¼″ ⅜″

⅜″

top

1¾″

Make 1 of each.
Label #1 and #2.

bottom

chassis

#2

Make hole for steering post.

top

¾″

#1

2¼″

¾″

Motor Bulkhead #2

front end

1″

Location of Motor
Bulkheads on Chassis

DIAGRAM 3
Nose Bulkheads

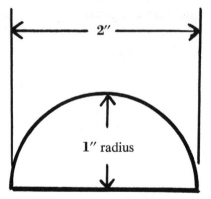

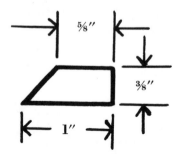

Top Nose Bulkhead #4
Make 1.

Nose Bulkheads #3 and #3A
Make 1 of each. Label #3 and #3A.

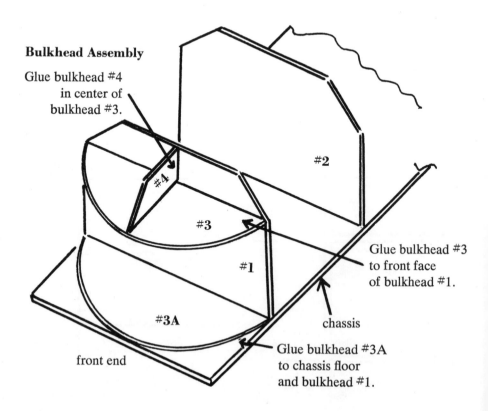

Bulkhead Assembly

Glue bulkhead #4
in center of
bulkhead #3.

#4

#2

#3

#1

Glue bulkhead #3
to front face
of bulkhead #1.

#3A

chassis

front end

Glue bulkhead #3A
to chassis floor
and bulkhead #1.

Top Nose Bulkhead #4 (Diagram 3)

Top nose bulkhead #4 supports the curved shape of the upper nose covering. Draw and cut it out from rigid cardboard as shown in Diagram 3. Glue the long end of bulkhead #4 down the center of the top side of bulkhead #3. To keep bulkhead #4 in a vertical position, glue its straight short edge to the center of bulkhead #1. See Diagram 3.

Main Motor Panel (Diagram 4)

The covering for the motor compartment is made from brown construction paper, or any color paper you wish. The covering is attached in three panels, beginning with the main motor panel. Draw and cut out this piece as shown in Diagram 4. Draw the line design on one side with pen and black ink. Bend the gluing tabs and two small upper panels toward the plain side.

The main motor panel extends from one side of bulkhead #2 around the curved nose bulkheads to the opposite side of bulkhead #2. Glue one of the end gluing tabs to the back of bulkhead #2 and the adjacent bottom gluing tab to the chassis. Carefully wrap the panel around the motor compartment bulkheads, keeping the bottom edge even with the chassis. Glue the panel to the edges of bulkheads #1, #3, and #3A as you proceed. Attach the opposite end of the panel to the chassis and bulkhead #2 as before. Glue the two small upper sections of the panel (they look like gluing tabs) to the slanted edges of bulkheads #1 and #2. See the photograph of the finished model on page 86. If certain sections of the panel do not fit properly, trim the edges with your knife or scissors.

Top Panel of Motor Hood (Diagram 5)

Draw and cut out the top panel as shown in Diagram 5. Draw the design on one side with pen and black ink. Glue the panel's straight edge to the exposed upper edge of bulkhead #2. Next glue the underside of the panel to the edge of the two small upper

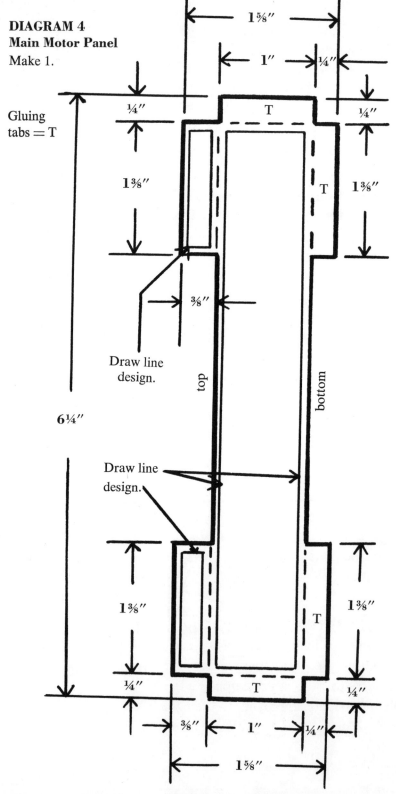

DIAGRAM 4
Main Motor Panel
Make 1.

Gluing
tabs = T

1⅝″

1″

¼″

¼″

T

¼″

1⅜″

T

1⅜″

6¼″

⅜″

Draw line
design.

top

bottom

Draw line
design.

1⅜″

1⅜″

T

¼″

T

¼″

⅜″

1″

¼″

1⅝″

sections of the main panel. Finally, glue the underside of the panel to the top edge of bulkhead #1 where the two pieces meet. Be sure to keep the top panel parallel to the chassis. The curved front end is not attached until the curved nose panel is in place.

Curved Nose Panel of Motor Hood (Diagram 5)

Draw and cut out the curved nose panel as shown in Diagram 5. Draw the design on one side with pen and black ink. Before gluing, place the panel in position between the top panel and the main motor panel to make sure it will fit perfectly. Trim any rough edges with your scissors.

DIAGRAM 5
Motor Hood Panels

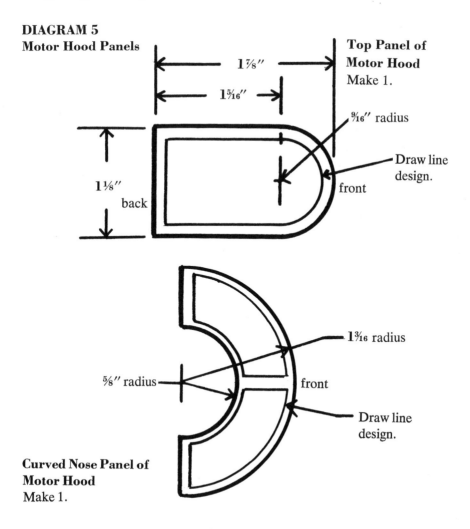

Top Panel of
Motor Hood
Make 1.

1⅞″

1⁵⁄₁₆″

⁹⁄₁₆″ radius

Draw line
design.

1⅛″
back

front

1¾₁₆ radius

⅝″ radius

front

Draw line
design.

Curved Nose Panel of
Motor Hood
Make 1.

First glue the center of the curved nose panel to the slanted edge of bulkhead #4. When this section is firmly attached, glue the entire bottom edge of the nose panel to the upper edge of the main motor panel. Finally, put glue along the nose panel's upper curved edge and press the loose front end of the top panel upon it. This seals and completes the motor compartment of the Stanley Steamer. As you proceed with this work, check the photograph of the finished model on page 111 often.

Rear Motor Wall (Diagram 6)

In addition to bulkhead #2, there is an extra, slightly larger rear wall to the Stanley Steamer's motor compartment. Draw and cut out this piece as shown in Diagram 6. Use rigid cardboard. Cover the piece with the same color construction paper you used for the motor compartment, or paint it with matching poster paint.

Make a small hole through the rear motor wall for the steering post as shown in Diagram 6. Use a sharp-pointed tool to begin the hole, then enlarge it with a pencil point. Make the hole just large enough for a length of large matchstick to slide through.

Glue the bottom edge of the rear motor wall to the chassis floor and the forward side to the back of bulkhead #2. Be sure the top and sides overhang the same amount all around. See the photograph of the finished model on page 86.

DIAGRAM 6
Rear Motor Wall
Make 1.

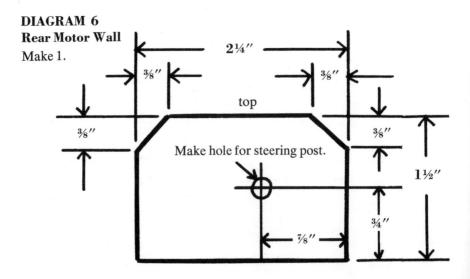

2¼"

⅜"   ⅜"

⅜"   top   ⅜"

Make hole for steering post.

1½"

¾"

⅞"

DIAGRAM 7
Dashboard
Make 1.

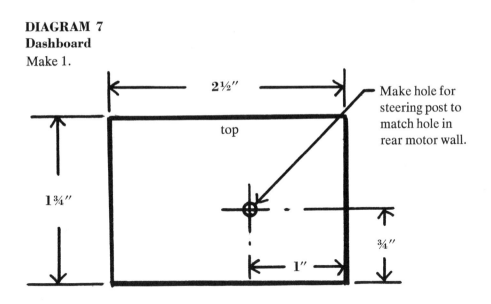

Dashboard (Diagram 7)

The dashboard is actually a third, even larger rear motor wall. Draw and cut out the dashboard from rigid cardboard as shown in Diagram 7. Cover the dashboard with light green or any color construction paper, or paint it with poster paint.

Make a hole in the dashboard for the steering post to match the hole in the rear motor wall. Now, once the gauges have been attached, the dashboard can be glued in place.

Gauges #1, #2, and #3 (Diagram 8)

Draw and cut out the gauges from black construction paper as shown in Diagram 8. Glue them in place on the dashboard as shown in Assembly Diagram 8. Try to keep the gauges exactly in line with one another.

After the gauges are firmly attached, glue the dashboard in place along its bottom edge and forward side. Press it firmly to the chassis floor and against the rear motor wall so the top and sides overhang the same amount all around. See the photograph of the finished model on page 118.

DIAGRAM 8
Gauges #1, #2, and #3

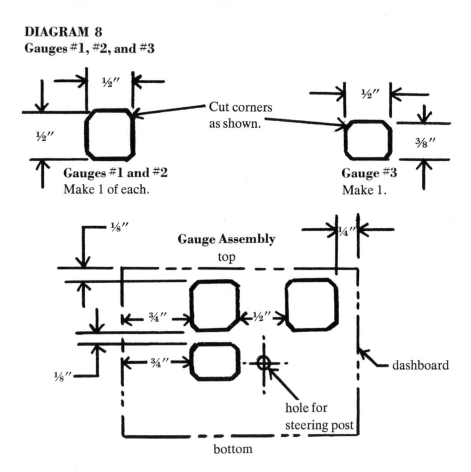

Cut corners as shown.

½″

½″

Gauges #1 and #2
Make 1 of each.

½″

⅜″

Gauge #3
Make 1.

⅛″

Gauge Assembly
top

¼″

¾″

½″

¾″

⅛″

dashboard

hole for
steering post

bottom

Side Body Panels (Diagram 9)

Compared to today's automobiles, the body of the Stanley Steamer was almost nothing. It served more as decoration than as protection for the driver.

Two side body panels are needed for this model. Draw and cut out these pieces as shown in Diagram 9. Use brown construction paper, or whatever color paper you used for the motor compartment. Draw the line design on opposite sides of the pieces for the right and left panels, using pen and black ink. Bend the gluing tabs along the dotted lines and away from the decorated side. The decorated side will face outward on your model.

Glue the side panels in place by first attaching the narrow end gluing tabs to the lower corners of the dashboard. Check to make

DIAGRAM 9
Side Body Panels
Make 2.

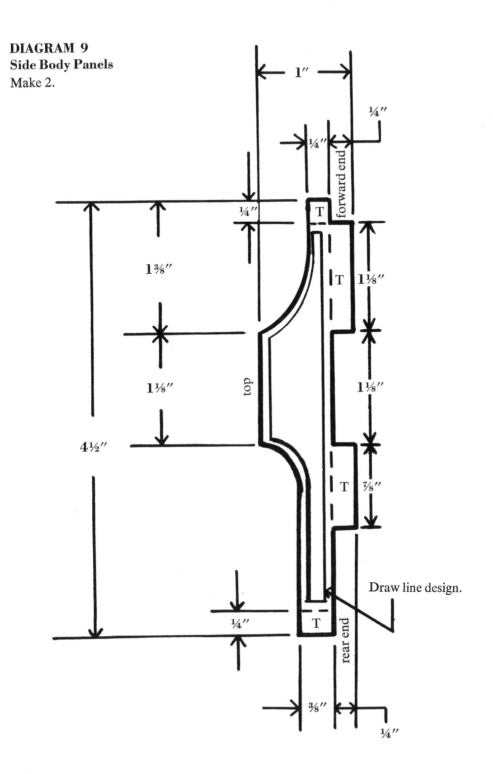

1″

¼″

¼″

¼″

1⅜″

forward end

T

T   1⅛″

1⅛″

top

1⅛″

4½″

T   ⅞″

Draw line design.

¼″

T

rear end

⅜″

¼″

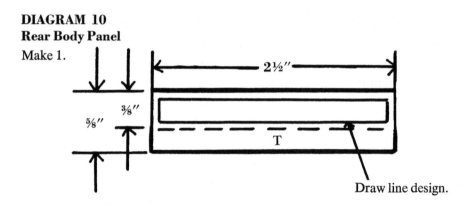

DIAGRAM 10
Rear Body Panel
Make 1.

2½″

⅜″

⅝″

T

Draw line design.

sure that the bottom edge of each panel is even with the chassis floor. Then glue the two bottom gluing tabs of each piece to the chassis floor. The back end gluing tabs will be attached to the rear body panel later. The side panels will seem rather weak at this point, but this is only temporary. As other units are made and attached, the panels will become quite sturdy.

Rear Body Panel (Diagram 10)

The rear body panel is a long, narrow piece with one gluing tab. Draw and cut it out as shown in Diagram 10. Use the same color construction paper you used for the side panels. Draw the design as shown on one side with pen and black ink. Bend the gluing tab away from the design side.

First glue the long gluing tab of the panel to the rear edge of the chassis. Be sure the edges of the panel and chassis are perfectly even. Next attach the two ends of the panel to the loose gluing tabs of the side body panels. The model now has a shallow enclosure from the driver's compartment to the tail end.

Seat Base (Diagram 11)

Designers of early cars firmly believed that the driver should be seated high for an unobstructed view of the road ahead. So the driver of the Stanley Steamer enjoyed a high perch. This consisted of a seat base with a seat on top.

100

Draw and cut out the seat base as shown in Diagram 11. Use the color construction paper you have chosen for your model. Be sure to score the dotted lines carefully so the seat base will have straight, square corners and edges. If any portion of it is crooked, everything attached to it will also be crooked. Fold along the scored lines to form a boxlike shape which is open at the bottom. Glue the four side tabs to hold.

Glue the tabs at the bottom of the seat base to the chassis floor between the two bottom tabs of each side body panel. See the photograph of the finished model on page 86. Glue the wide center section of the side panels to the ends of the seat base where these pieces connect. This attachment will make the side body panels quite sturdy.

DIAGRAM 11
Seat Base
Make 1.

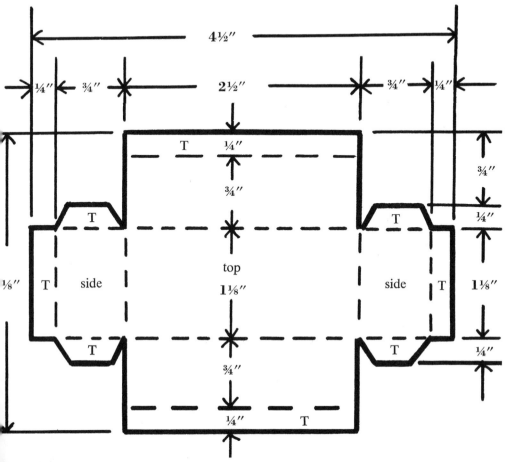

DIAGRAM 12

Top of Seat Base
Make 1.

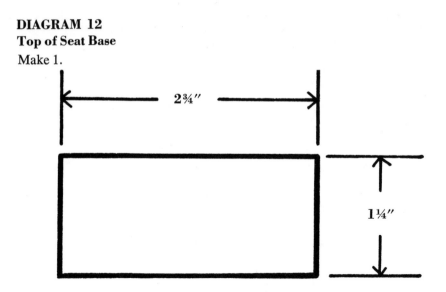

Top of Seat Base (Diagram 12)

An extra top piece made from rigid cardboard is attached to the seat base. This will be the base for the driver's seat.

Draw and cut out the piece as shown in Diagram 12. Cover it with the same color construction paper you used to make the seat base, or paint it with matching poster paint. Glue the rectangle to the top of the seat base. It has a slight overhang on all four edges.

Side Seat Panels (Diagram 13)

The first parts of the seat to be made are the side panels. Draw and cut out these pieces as shown in Diagram 13. Use the same color construction paper you used to make the seat base. Score and fold along the dotted lines, bending the gluing tabs for the right and left panels in opposite directions. Set the side panels aside until the back seat panel, cushion for the back seat panel, and cushions for the side seat panels have been made.

Back Seat Panel (Diagram 13)

When the seat is finally assembled, the back seat panel will connect the two side panels. Draw and cut out this piece as shown in Diagram 13. Use the same color construction paper you used for the side panels. Set aside with the side seat panels.

DIAGRAM 13
Seat Panels

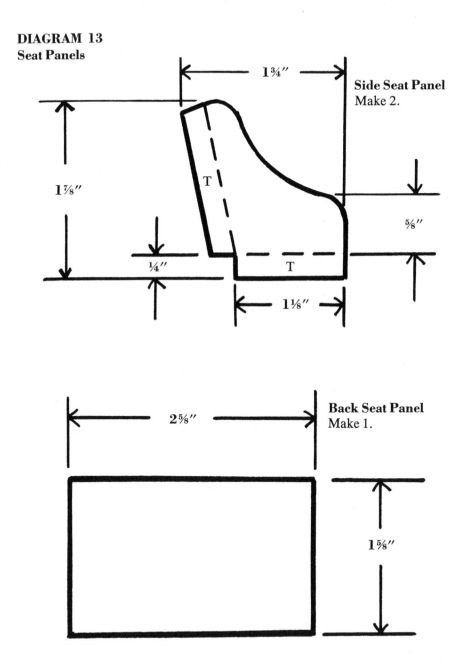

Cushion for Back Seat Panel (Diagram 14)

The cushion for the back seat panel is the same size as the panel. Draw and cut out the cushion pattern from yellow construction paper. Draw the cushion design on one side, using pen and black drawing ink. Glue the cushion panel to the back seat panel, laying both parts flat on your work surface. All four edges of both pieces should match perfectly. Set aside again with the side seat panels.

Cushions for Side Seat Panels (Diagram 14)

The cushion for the side seat panels is also an exact copy, minus the gluing tabs, of the panels themselves. Draw and cut out these pieces from yellow construction paper as shown in Diagram 14. (You may instead trace the cushion outline from the side seat panels that you have already made [Diagram 12].) Draw the cushion design on one side of each piece, using pen and black drawing ink. The design should be on opposite sides for the right and left panels.

Lay the side seat panels flat on your work surface with the tabs pointing upward. Match the cushions with the side panels and glue each pair together. Trim any overhang with your scissors. Now the seat is ready to be assembled and glued.

Seat Assembly

The side seat panels are attached to the top of the seat base first. Place each panel on the seat base so that the fold edge of the short gluing tab is even with the edge of the seat base. Glue the tabs to the base. Place the back seat panel between the long gluing tabs on the side seat panels. The top and bottom edges of the back seat panel should be even with the top and bottom edges of the side seat panels. Glue the long gluing tabs to the back of the back seat panel. Make sure that the seat corners, where the back and side panels meet, are straight and do not have gaps. If the corners are crooked, it will be difficult to install the seat cushion.

DIAGRAM 14
Back and Side Cushions

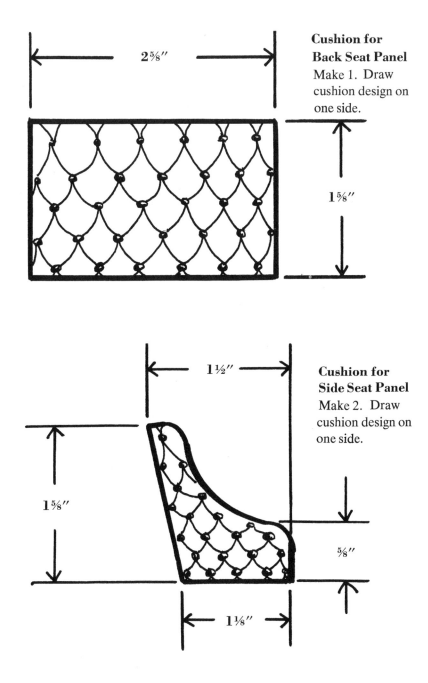

2⅝″

Cushion for
Back Seat Panel
Make 1. Draw
cushion design on
one side.

1⅝″

1½″

Cushion for
Side Seat Panel
Make 2. Draw
cushion design on
one side.

1⅝″

⅝″

1⅛″

DIAGRAM 15
Seat Cushion

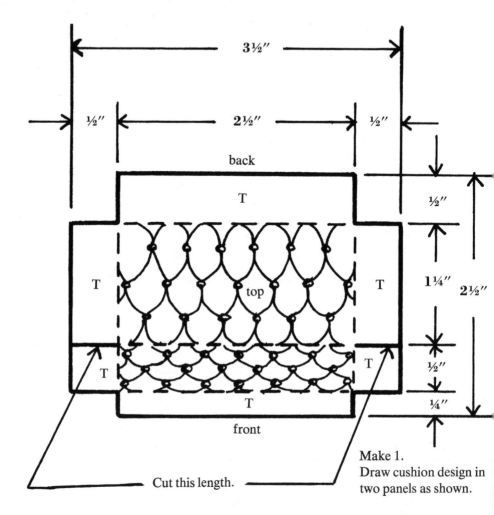

3½″

½″   2½″   ½″

back

T

½″

T   top   T   1¼″   2½″

T   T   ½″

T

front   ¼″

Make 1.
Draw cushion design in
two panels as shown.

Cut this length.

Seat Cushion (Diagram 15)

A seat cushion completes the seat assembly. Draw and cut out
the seat cushion as shown in Diagram 15, using yellow construction paper. Draw the cushion design on the two panels as shown
with pen and black drawing ink. Score and fold along the dotted
lines to make a boxlike unit which is open at the bottom. Glue
the cushion together at the corner tabs.

106

Place the cushion in position on the seat base between the two side panels to make sure it fits properly. If any adjustment is needed, do it at this point. The bottom edge of the decorated panel facing forward should be even with the front edge of the top of the seat base. See the photograph of the finished model on page 86. Glue the cushion in place along the four long gluing tabs. Press down on the cushion for a few minutes to make sure it is firmly attached.

Toolbox (Diagram 16)
Drivers of early cars always took along a box full of tools and spare parts. They never knew when the engine would wheeze and die or a tire would flatten.

Draw and cut out the toolbox of the Stanley Steamer as shown in Diagram 16. Use the same color construction paper you used for the motor compartment. Carefully score and fold along the dotted lines to form a rectangular box which is open at the top. Glue the box together along the four gluing tabs.

The top of the toolbox is a separate piece. Draw and cut out the cover as shown in Diagram 16. Use the same color color construction paper you used for the body of the box. Carefully score along the dotted lines and fold to form the lid. Glue together at the corner tabs. Fit and glue the cover to the top of the box. Then glue the entire toolbox to the back end of the car body, about ¼ inch from the rear panel and equally spaced from both sides. See the photograph of the finished model on page 118.

Foot Brake and Throttle (Diagram 17)
Draw and cut out the foot brake and throttle as shown in Diagram 17. Use rigid cardboard and paint each piece with yellow poster paint. Glue the brake and throttle at an angle so the top edges are attached to the dashboard and the bottom edges are attached to the chassis floor. See Assembly Diagram 17, and the photograph of the finished model on page 118.

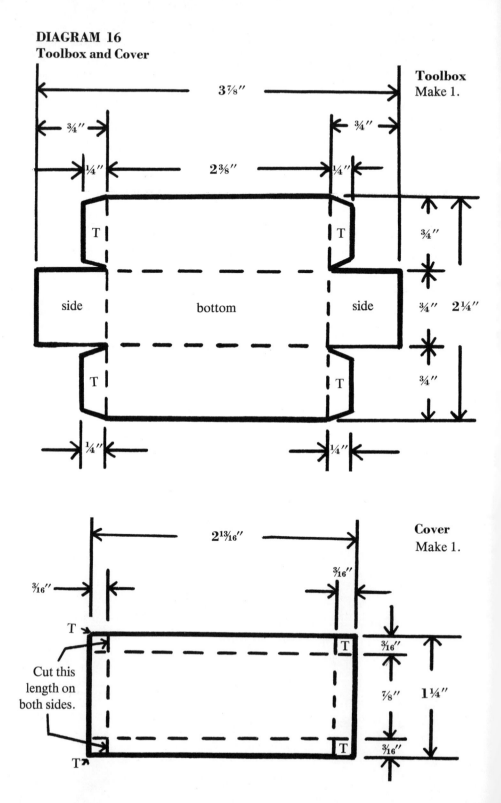

DIAGRAM 16
Toolbox and Cover

Toolbox
Make 1.

3⅞″

¾″ · 2⅜″ · ¾″

¼″ · ¼″

T · T

¾″

side · bottom · side · ¾″ · 2¼″

T · T · ¾″

¼″ · ¼″

Cover
Make 1.

2¹³⁄₁₆″

³⁄₁₆″ · ³⁄₁₆″

T · T · ³⁄₁₆″

Cut this
length on
both sides.

⅞″ · 1¼″

T · ³⁄₁₆″

T

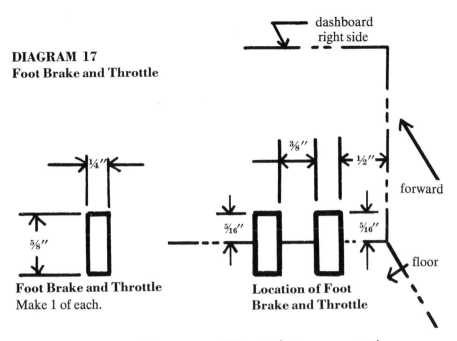

DIAGRAM 17
Foot Brake and Throttle

dashboard
right side

¾″

½″

¼″

forward

⁵⁄₁₆″

⁵⁄₁₆″

⅝″

floor

Foot Brake and Throttle
Make 1 of each.

Location of Foot
Brake and Throttle

Steering Post and Steering Wheel (Diagram 18)

The steering post for the Stanley Steamer model is a 4-inch length of large matchstick wood with one end cut at an angle. Cut as shown in Diagram 18. Paint the steering post with yellow poster paint.

Cut the steering wheel from rigid cardboard, following Diagram 18. Draw the spokes and rim as shown on both sides of the wheel, using pen and black ink.

To join the steering wheel and post, lay the wheel flat on your work surface. Put a generous amount of glue in its center. Let the glue dry for a few minutes and become tacky. Press the squared-off end of the steering post into the glue so that the wheel and post form a perfect right angle. See Assembly Diagram 18.

The steering wheel unit is inserted through the two matched holes in the dashboard and rear motor wall. Before doing this, push the point of your pencil through the holes, turning it if necessary, to make sure the holes are aligned and are large enough for the steering post to fit through.

Then put a generous amount of glue on the slanted end of the steering post, and slide it through the two holes at an angle until you can feel it touching the chassis inside the motor compartment. Hold the steering post for a few minutes until it stays in place by

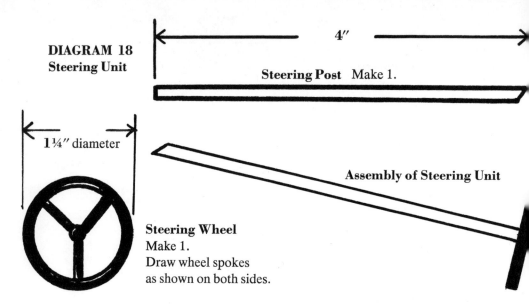

DIAGRAM 18
Steering Unit

4″

Steering Post Make 1.

1¼″ diameter

Assembly of Steering Unit

Steering Wheel
Make 1.
Draw wheel spokes
as shown on both sides.

itself. Then put a generous amount of glue around the dashboard opening. Once this hardens, the steering wheel unit will be extremely secure.

Windshield (Diagram 19)

The windshield of the model of the Stanley Steamer is made from lengths of round toothpick and large matchstick wood. The large matchstick pieces form the top and bottom of the windshield frame. Cut the frame parts to the lengths shown in Diagram 19.

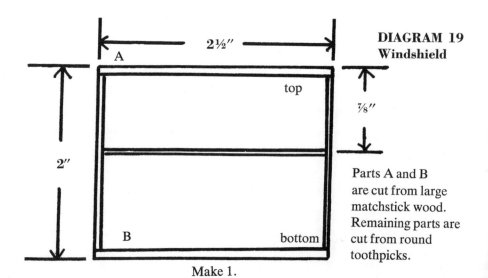

2½″

A

top

DIAGRAM 19
Windshield

⅞″

2″

B

bottom

Parts A and B
are cut from large
matchstick wood.
Remaining parts are
cut from round
toothpicks.

Make 1.

Assemble the cut pieces on a flat wood board or stiff shiny card-board, following the pattern in Diagram 19. Put a generous amount of glue at each joint of the frame. After about half an hour, or just before the glue has hardened, slide the edge of your knife under each glued joint to pry them loose from the wood or cardboard surface. Look at the frame sideways to make sure that the unit is flat and square. Adjust any askew pieces, then carefully put the unit aside. When the glue has thoroughly hardened, paint the windshield black.

The firmly-glued windshield is attached to the top edge of the dashboard. Put a generous amount of glue along this top edge. Let the glue dry for ten or fifteen minutes until it becomes quite tacky. Press the bottom edge of the windshield into the glue, so that the windshield corners are even with the corners of the dash-board. Examine the windshield-dashboard unit sideways to make sure it is perfectly vertical. Hold the dashboard in position for a few minutes. Because of the tackiness of the glue, the windshield should remain upright after you release it.

DIAGRAM 20
Side Frames of Roof

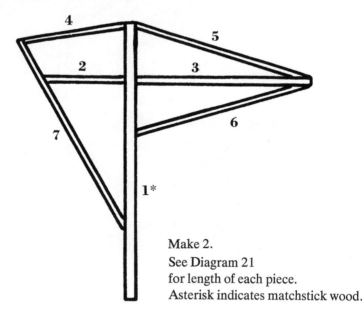

Make 2.
See Diagram 21
for length of each piece.
Asterisk indicates matchstick wood.

Side Frames of Roof (Diagrams 20-21)

The motor compartment and the roof of this model are the most complicated units to construct. The roof consists of two side frames joined by matchstick crosspieces which are covered with black construction paper.

The two side frames of the roof are made from lengths of round toothpick and large matchstick wood. Draw the pattern of the frames as shown in Diagram 20 on a flat piece of wood or stiff shiny cardboard. Number each length as shown. Cut the toothpick and matchstick wood to the length given for each numbered piece in Diagram 21. It is best to work on just one frame at a time. Place each cut length on its numbered position on the pattern.

When all the pieces have been put in place, they can be removed one by one for gluing. Put a generous amount of glue on the ends of each piece, except for the matchstick in the center.

DIAGRAM 21
Lengths of Roof Frame Parts

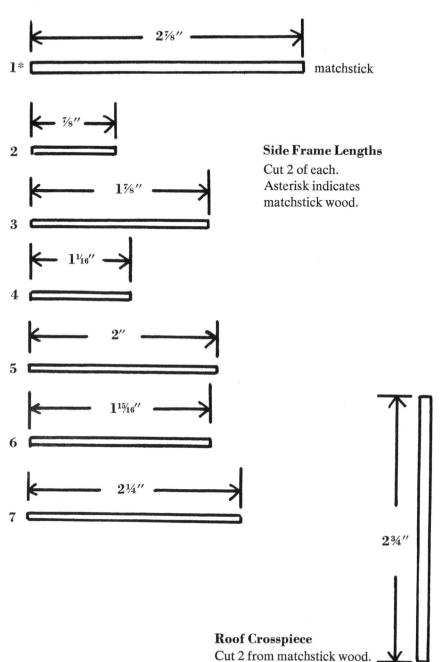

1* ⊢——— 2⅞″ ———⊣   matchstick

2 ⊢ ⅞″ ⊣

Side Frame Lengths
Cut 2 of each.
Asterisk indicates
matchstick wood.

3 ⊢——— 1⅞″ ———⊣

4 ⊢ 1¹⁄₁₆″ ⊣

5 ⊢——— 2″ ———⊣

6 ⊢——— 1¹⁵⁄₁₆″ ———⊣

7 ⊢——— 2¼″ ———⊣

2¾″

Roof Crosspiece
Cut 2 from matchstick wood.

Set the frame aside to dry for about half an hour. Then slide your craft knife under each glued joint while the glue is still tacky. Twist your knife slightly to pry the joints free of the work surface. Look at the frame sideways to make sure that all the pieces are straight and properly aligned. Adjust any crooked pieces, then set the frame aside so the glue can completely harden. In the meantime, make the second frame, following the same procedure.

Roof Crosspieces (Diagram 21)

The side frames are joined by two crosspieces made from large matchstick wood. Cut these pieces to the length given in Diagram 21.

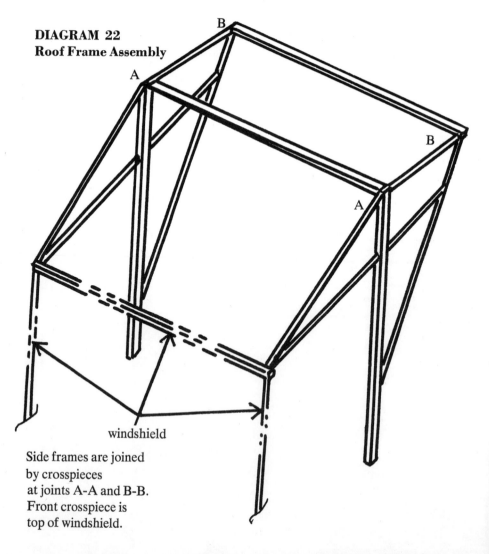

DIAGRAM 22
Roof Frame Assembly

windshield

Side frames are joined
by crosspieces
at joints A-A and B-B.
Front crosspiece is
top of windshield.

Roof Frame Assembly (Diagram 22)

The roof frame unit is completed by joining the side frames with the two crosspieces at joints A-A and B-B. See Assembly Diagram 22. This is easy to do if you turn the frames upside down. It does not matter which crosspiece is glued in place first. Put a generous amount of glue on the ends of each crosspiece, and press into position on the side frames. While the glue is drying, place supports on both sides of the frames to keep them upright. Use erasers, bottles of paint, or whatever else you have handy.

After the glue has thoroughly dried, paint the roof frame with black poster paint. You may be wondering why the forward end of the roof frame has no crosspiece. Eventually, when the completed roof is installed on the car model, the forward support will be provided by the top of the windshield. See Diagram 22.

Side Roof Panels (Diagram 23)

Now that the frame is complete, the roof covering can be added. On this model of the Stanley Steamer, the roof covering consists of four panels: one top, one back, and two side. The side panels are installed first.

Draw and cut out these side roof panels as shown in Diagram 23. Use black construction paper. Score along the dotted lines to make neat, straight folds for the gluing tabs. Be sure that the gluing tabs on the right and left panels bend in opposite directions.

DIAGRAM 23
Side Roof Panels
Make 2.

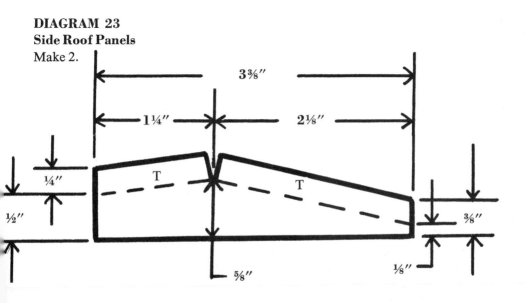

Place the panels in position on the frame to make sure they fit properly. Trim away any overhang with your scissors or knife. Bend the gluing tabs over the top edges of the frame, but leave them loose. Instead, glue the side panels in place along the sides of the roof frame, wherever the two pieces connect. The gluing tabs will be used later for attaching the top roof panel.

Top Roof Panel (Diagram 24)

Draw and cut out the top roof panel from black construction paper as shown in Diagram 24. Lightly score along the dotted lines, being especially careful along the center crease. Bend the back gluing tab firmly, but only crease the center so that the top roof panel follows the curve of the frame.

Place the top roof panel on the frame to make sure it fits properly. Then glue the side edges to the gluing tabs of the side panels. Next glue the back end to the top of the back crosspiece. Glue the

DIAGRAM 24
Top Roof Panel

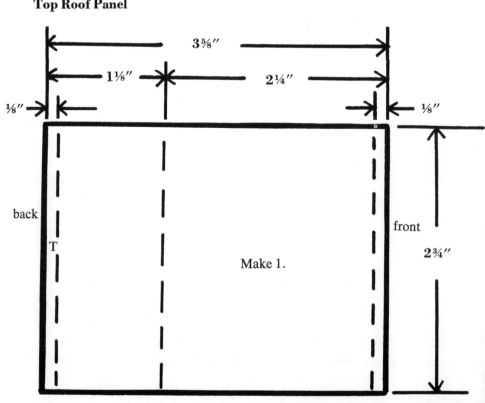

narrow back gluing tab to the back of the roof frame, near the top corners. The narrow strip at the front of the top roof panel will be glued in place after the entire roof unit has been installed on the car model.

Back Roof Panel (Diagram 25)

The back panel of the roof is a simple rectangle with two oval windows glued to each side. Draw and cut it out from black construction paper as shown in Diagram 25. For the windows, draw and cut out four ovals from white construction paper and glue two to each side of the rectangle. See Diagram 25 for their size and position.

Glue the top edge of the back panel to the back of the roof frame. The top edge of the back panel should be even with the top edge of the rear crosspiece. The bottom of the back panel is left loose until the roof unit has been attached to the car model.

DIAGRAM 25
Back Roof Panel

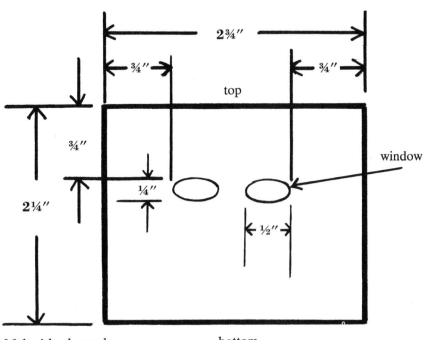

2¾″

¾″   ¾″

top

¾″

window

2¼″   ¼″

½″

Make 1 back panel.   bottom
Make 4 oval windows.

Installing the Roof

To attach the roof unit, first glue the matchstick supports of the side frames to the inner sides of the seat, near the corners. See the photograph of the finished model on page 86. Then bend the narrow strip at the front of the top roof panel downward. Glue this strip to the front edge of the top of the windshield. Now glue the loose end of the back panel of the roof to the back of the seat near the top. The completed roof back should slant to the rear. See the photograph of the finished model on this page.

Running Board Back Splashes (Diagram 26)

On early cars, like the Stanley Steamer, running boards were placed outside the body, not inside as on modern automobiles. Part of the running board unit was a guard piece, which we call a back splash, that prevented stones and mud from flying up onto the running board. There was a running board unit on each side of the car.

Draw and cut out the back splashes as shown in Diagram 26. Use black construction paper. Carefully score and fold along the dotted lines to form the steplike shape shown in Diagram 26. Glue side A of each back splash to the underside of the chassis, one on each side. Side A should be even with the chassis edge along the fold, and even with the dashboard at the front edge. See the photograph of the finished model on page 86. Side C will be attached to the underside of the running board later.

DIAGRAM 26
Running Board Back Splashes
Make 2.

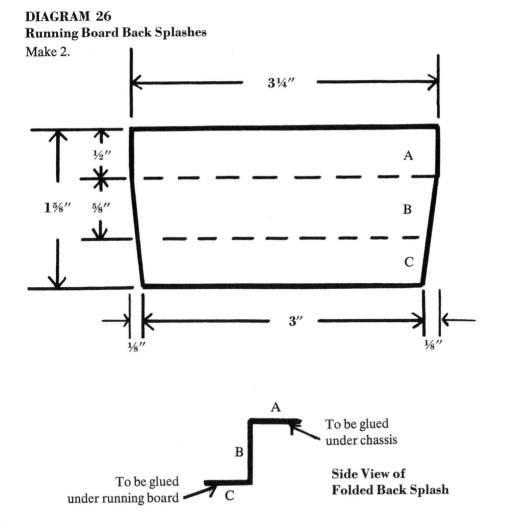

Side View of
Folded Back Splash

DIAGRAM 27

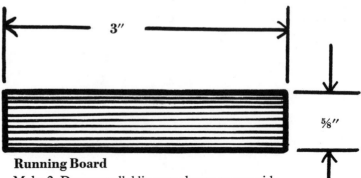

Running Board
Make 2. Draw parallel lines as shown on one side.

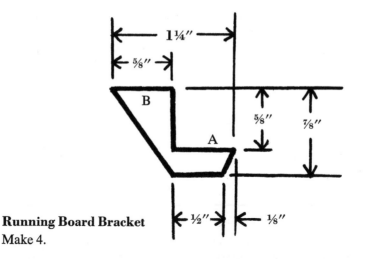

Running Board Bracket
Make 4.

Running Boards (Diagram 27)

Draw and cut out the running boards as shown in Diagram 27. Use rigid cardboard. Draw the parallel lines as shown on one side of each running board, using pen and black drawing ink. Glue one running board, design side upward, to side C of each back splash. See the photograph of the finished model on page 111.

Running Board Brackets (Diagram 27)

Two brackets are attached to the underside of each running board to provide support in addition to the back splash. Draw and cut out the four brackets as shown in Diagram 27. Use rigid cardboard. Paint the brackets with black poster paint.

Turn the car model upside down for positioning and gluing the bracket supports. Glue two brackets along edge A to the underside of each running board, placing them ¾ inch from the front and back edges. Glue edge B of each bracket to side A of the back splash on the underside of the chassis. Before the glue hardens, make certain that the brackets are in a vertical position.

Wheels (Diagram 28)

Draw and cut out the four wheels, following Diagram 28. Use rigid cardboard that is not too thick so you can cut it easily with your scissors. Draw the spokes and tire design as shown on both sides of each wheel. Use pen and black drawing ink.

DIAGRAM 28
Wheels

2″ diameter

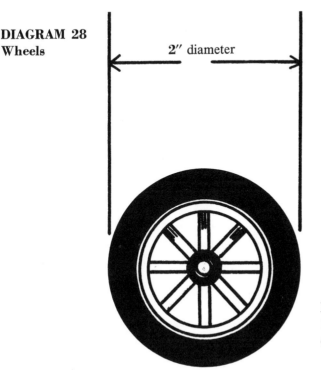

Make 4.
Draw wheel design
on both sides.

Wheel Boxes (Diagram 29)

A wheel box is glued in the center of each wheel, and is used to connect the wheels to the axles. Draw and cut out the four wheel boxes, following Diagram 29. Use black construction paper.

Mark and cut an "X" in the center of each pattern with the point of your knife, as shown in Diagram 29. Since the ends of the axles will be inserted through these openings, do not make them too large. The wheel-axle connection should be a snug fit.

Score and fold along the dotted lines very carefully so the boxes have straight, sharp edges which will fit squarely on the wheels. Assemble each one into a boxlike shape which is open on one side. Glue together at the corner gluing tabs. Attach a wheel box to the exact center of one side of each wheel. Glue the box to the wheel along the gluing tabs of the open side. Put a small weight on each box, such as a bottle of poster paint, until the glue hardens. Set aside until the axles have been made.

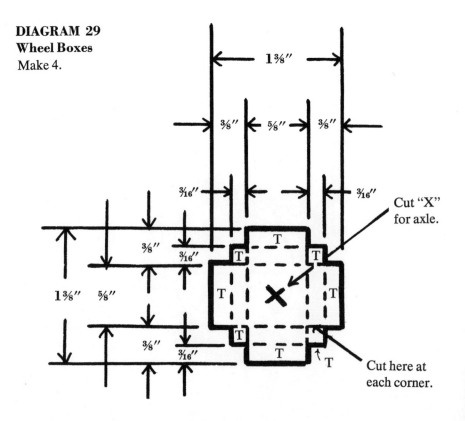

DIAGRAM 29
Wheel Boxes
Make 4.

Leaf Springs (Diagram 30)

There are four spring units on the model of the Stanley Steamer. Each unit consists of two leaf springs, two pins, and one separator.

Draw and cut out the eight leaf springs as shown in Diagram 30. Use rigid cardboard. Draw the leaf spring design as shown on both sides of each piece with pen and black drawing ink.

The leaf springs of each unit are connected by two small pins sandwiched between them, one at each end. Cut the eight pins from a length of round toothpick to the size shown in Diagram 30. Paint the pins with black poster paint. Glue one pin lengthwise to each end of one leaf spring. Put a generous amount of glue on top of these pins. Position the second leaf spring directly above the first, and press the ends onto the glued pins. Hold the unit together at both ends either by tying string around them or by clamping them together with a metal spring-type hair clip. It is very important that the two leaf springs be firmly connected. Repeat for the three remaining spring units.

The separator for each unit pushes the leaf springs apart to give them a wide double V-shape. Draw and cut out the four separators as shown in Diagram 30. Use rigid cardboard and paint them black. Insert the separator for each unit while the ends of the leaf springs are still tied or clamped. Put glue on the narrow ends of the separator and slide it between the leaf springs. Turn the separator upright in the exact center of the leaf springs, which is marked by the small circle in the leaf spring design. The long sides of the separator should be even with the sides of the leaf springs. See Assembly Diagram 30. The separator will be extremely tight. Make certain that it is in a vertical position between the leaf springs.

When all four spring units are completed, they can be glued to the chassis of the car model. The spring units extend halfway beyond the front and rear ends of the chassis at all four corners. The best way to attach the spring units is to turn the car model upside down. Put a generous amount of glue on the small circle on one side of each spring unit. Glue one spring unit to each

123

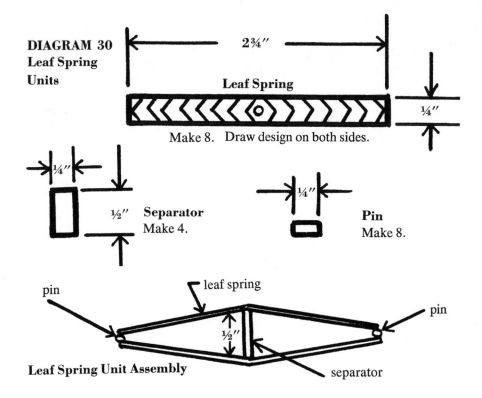

DIAGRAM 30
Leaf Spring
Units

2¾″

Leaf Spring

¼″

Make 8. Draw design on both sides.

¼″

½″ Separator
Make 4.

¼″

Pin
Make 8.

pin

leaf spring

pin

½″

Leaf Spring Unit Assembly

separator

corner of the chassis. Make sure that the long sides of the spring units are even with the long sides of the chassis. Also make sure that the separators are at right angles to the chassis so that the leaf springs are in a perfectly horizontal position.

Axles (Diagram 31)

The two axles for the Stanley Steamer model are made from large matchstick wood. Cut the axles to the length given in Diagram 31 and paint them with the yellow poster paint.

Begin the wheel-axle assembly by attaching one wheel to one end of each axle end. To do this, put a large amount of glue on the axle end or in the slotted opening of the wheel box. Allow the glue to dry for a few minutes and become tacky before you insert the axle into the wheel box. Make sure that the axle is at a perfect right angle to the wheel so your finished model will not be lopsided. One way of checking this is to stand your ruler in a vertical position close to the axle. Turn the wheel to all four sides of the

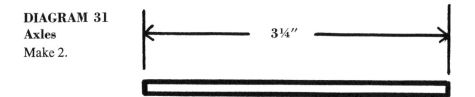

DIAGRAM 31
Axles
Make 2.

3¼″

wheel box and adjust the axle so it is parallel to the straight edge of the ruler on each side.

Before attaching the second wheel to each axle, turn the car model upside down. Slide one axle between the rear leaf springs behind the separators. Slide the other axle between the front leaf springs in front of the separators. Now glue the remaining wheels to the free axle ends. Put lots of glue in the slotted openings of the wheel boxes and press the boxes onto the axle ends. Use both hands to press both wheels on each axle. Make sure each axle end is glued all the way into the wheel box openings.

Finally, attach the wheel-axle assemblies to the spring units at the joints formed by the separators and bottom leaf springs. Put a generous amount of glue on the axle side of the separators and the upper surface of the bottom leaf springs, and press the axles in place. Adjust the wheels so that they are the same distance from the sides of the chassis and even with the back and front edges of the car model. Keep the model turned upside down until the glue has thoroughly dried. Once the axles are attached, you are coming down the homestretch toward your finished Stanley Steamer model.

Front Fenders (Diagram 32)

Draw and cut out the two front fenders as shown in Diagram 32. Use black construction paper. Before the fenders are attached, they must be bent in two places. Make the first by sharply folding along the dotted lines of the short rear gluing tab. The second is a gentle curve which will be above each front wheel. See the photograph of the finished model on page 86. To make the second bend, draw the front half of each fender lightly over the edge of

125

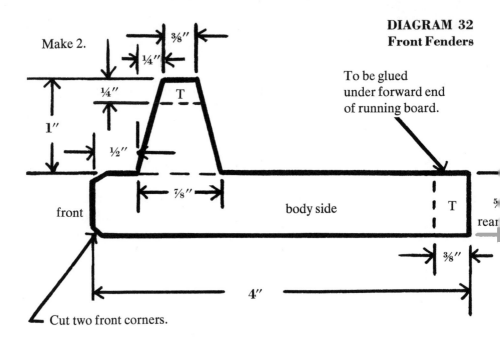

DIAGRAM 32
Front Fenders

Make 2.

⅜″

¼″

¼″

1″

½″

T

⅞″

front

body side

T

rear

To be glued
under forward end
of running board.

⅜″

4″

Cut two front corners.

your work surface or ruler. Be sure to curve opposite sides for the right and left fenders. Be careful not to make these bends too sharp.

The front fenders have two attachment points—under the running board and at the front end of the chassis. Glue the rear gluing tab of each front fender to the underside of the running board first. Be sure the front support tabs are on the sides next to the motor compartment. Bend these supports in a modified L-shape, so that the gluing tabs rest on top of the chassis. The curved portion of each fender should be about ¼ inch above the wheel. Glue the gluing tabs of the front supports to the chassis.

Rear Fenders (Diagram 33)

The rear fenders have a slightly different shape and curve from the front fenders. Draw and cut out the two rear fenders from black construction paper as shown in Diagram 33. Draw the front half of each fender over the edge of your work surface or ruler to curve it. Be sure to curve opposite sides for the right and left fenders. See the photograph of the finished model on page 86.

Bend each short gluing tab so it is at a right angle to the curved

126

DIAGRAM 33
Rear Fenders
Make 2.

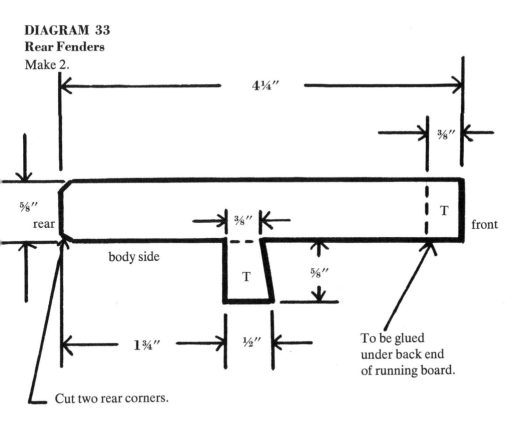

4¼″

⅜″

⅝″

rear

body side

T

⅜″

⅝″

T

front

1¾″

½″

To be glued
under back end
of running board.

Cut two rear corners.

fender. Glue the tabs to the underside of the back end of the running boards. Make sure the side fender supports are next to the body. Glue these side supports directly to the sides of the body at the rear corners so that the fenders are about ¼ inch above the rear wheels. See the photograph of the finished model on page 86.

Carriage Lamps (Diagram 34)

Two carriage lamps attached to the corners of the dashboard gave the Stanley Steamer an elegant look. Draw and cut out these lamps as shown in Diagram 34. Use yellow construction paper. Draw the windows as accurately as possible with pen and black drawing ink. Carefully score and bend along the dotted lines to give sharp, neat edges to the lamps' boxlike shapes. Assemble the lamps and glue together with the tabs on the inside.

Each carriage lamp has a top and bottom post. Cut these from round toothpicks to the lengths shown in Diagram 34. Paint the posts black. Attach the top posts first. Put a generous amount of glue in the center of the top side of each lamp. Let the glue dry for a few minutes and become tacky. Then attach the posts in a vertical position to the center of the glued sides.

As soon as the top posts are firmly glued, turn the carriage lamps upside down. Since the lamps cannot rest on the top posts, support each lamp on the edge of two small boxes, sliding the top post in between them. Or use a small bottle with the top post extending down through its neck. Once the lamps are properly supported, glue the bottom posts in place the same way you attached the top ones. Again, make certain that they are centered and straight.

The carriage lamps are attached to the outer upper corners of the dashboard. The tops of the lamps are even with the top edge of the dashboard, and the sides extend halfway out from the car body. See the photograph of the finished model on page 86. Put a generous amount of glue on one half of the rear side of each lamp, and press them into position. This is one of the few times when you will have to hold the parts in place until the glue hardens. Be patient—it really does not take too long.

DIAGRAM 34
Carriage Lamps

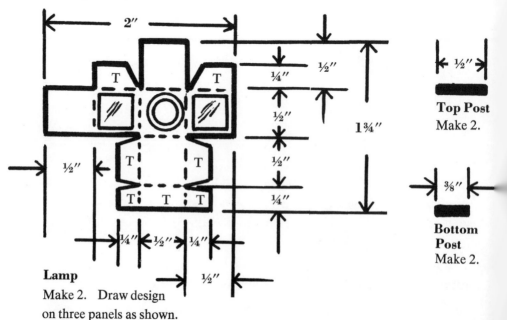

Lamp
Make 2. Draw design
on three panels as shown.

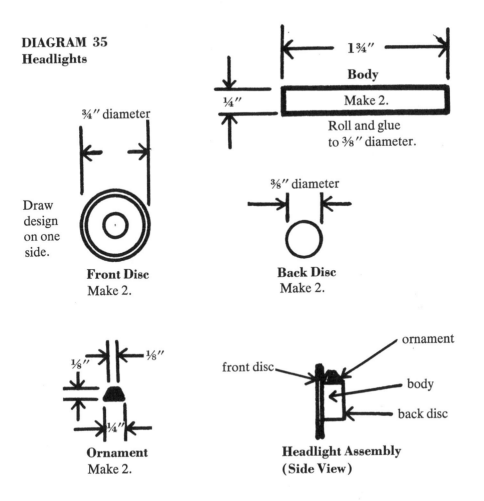

DIAGRAM 35
Headlights

¾″ diameter

Draw
design
on one
side.

Front Disc
Make 2.

1¾″

Body

Make 2.

¼″

Roll and glue
to ⅜″ diameter.

⅜″ diameter

Back Disc
Make 2.

⅛″   ⅛″

¼″

Ornament
Make 2.

ornament

front disc

body

back disc

Headlight Assembly
(Side View)

Headlights (Diagram 35)

In addition to the carriage lamps, the Stanley Steamer had two headlights. These were located on the front corners of the chassis.

Draw and cut out the body of the headlights, following Diagram 35. Use yellow construction paper. To make the cylindrical body shape, slide each piece lengthwise over the edge of your work surface or ruler to curve it. Now roll each piece into a cylinder ⅜ inch in diameter and glue it closed. If the glued ends overlap too much, trim away the excess on the inside of the cylinder with your scissors.

One end of the headlight body is closed by a disc. Draw and

129

cut these out as shown in Diagram 35. Use yellow construction paper. Glue it to one end of the body cylinder. The disc side is the back of the headlight.

The glass front and rim of each headlight is made from white construction paper. Draw and cut out the headlight front discs as shown in Diagram 35. Draw the rim design on one side of each disc with pen and black ink. Glue the plain side of the disc to the open end of the headlight body.

On the top of each headlight body is a small ornament. Draw and cut out this piece as shown in Diagram 35. Use rigid cardboard and paint each ornament black. Glue the ornaments to the top of the headlight bodies as shown in Assembly Diagram 35. Then glue the bottom of each headlight body to a corner of the front end of the chassis. See the photograph of the finished model on page 118.

Taillight (Diagram 36)

The Stanley Steamer model has one taillight. Draw and cut out the taillight body as shown in Diagram 36. Use yellow construction paper. Draw the piece lengthwise over the edge of your work surface or ruler to curl it. Roll the curled piece into a cylinder ⅜ inch in diameter and glue it closed. If the ends overlap too much, trim away the excess on the inside of the cylinder with your scissors.

DIAGRAM 36
Taillight

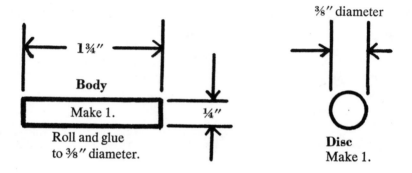

One end of the cylinder is covered with a disc. Draw and cut out the disc as shown in Diagram 36, using bright red construction paper. Glue the disc onto either end of the cylinder.

Place the taillight on top of the left rear leaf spring so that the open end is pressed against the rear side of the back body panel. See the photograph of the finished model on page 118. Glue the taillight to the left spring and body panel.

DIAGRAM 37
Hand Brake

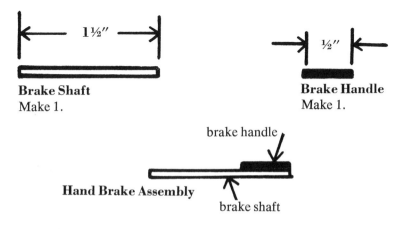

Hand Brake (Diagram 37)
The hand brake consists of two parts—a shaft and a handle. Both pieces are made from lengths of round toothpick. Cut both to the size given in Diagram 37. Paint the brake shaft yellow, using poster paint. Paint the brake handle black.

Glue the handle to the upper part of the shaft as shown in Assembly Diagram 37. Then glue the hand brake unit to the right-hand side of the model near the driver's seat, and at a slight rearward slant. See the photograph of the finished car model on page 118.

Tank (Diagram 38)
The Stanley Steamer was equipped with a tank which contained

131

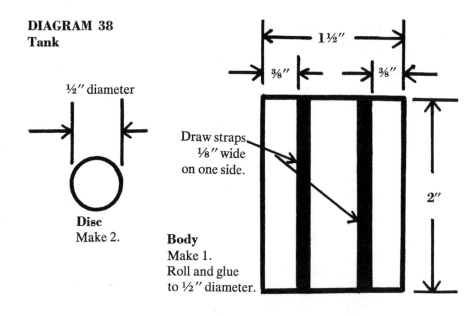

DIAGRAM 38
Tank

½" diameter

Disc
Make 2.

Draw straps
⅛" wide
on one side.

Body
Make 1.
Roll and glue
to ½" diameter.

1½"

⅜"   ⅜"

2"

gas for lighting the headlights. Almost all early cars had similar tanks.

Draw and cut out the tank body as shown in Diagram 38. Use yellow construction paper. Draw the two straps as shown on one side with pen and black drawing ink.

Pull the plain side of the tank body lengthwise over the edge of your work surface or ruler to curl it. Then roll the paper into a cylinder ½ inch in diameter. Glue the ends closed. If the ends overlap too much on the inside of the cylinder, trim the excess with your scissors.

Both ends of the tank are covered with yellow construction paper discs. Draw and cut out these pieces as shown in Diagram 38. Glue the discs to the ends of the tank.

Glue the completed tank horizontally to the right running board so that it rests against the back splash directly beneath the hand brake. See the photograph of the finished car model on page 86. Your Stanley Streamer model is now complete and ready for display at antique car rallies!

132

Chevrolet: 1915

Louis Chevrolet was part of the human flood of Europeans who came to the United States at the turn of this century to seek a better life. He was twenty-two and a highly skilled mechanic when he left his native Switzerland. He had already invented a new type of wine pump which had a great deal to do with his decision to emigrate to America. Louis believed it would be easier to sell his invention there than in his native land. However, as it turned out, it was the automobile, not the wine pump, that ultimately brought him good fortune.

During the early 1900s, the automobile was making news almost daily. It was mainly through newspaper stories that Louis Chevrolet became interested in and then associated with the motor car. He started his automotive career as a driver of powerful, fast racing cars.

During the pioneer years of the automobile's development, racing competitions were enormously popular. They were financially rewarding not only to daring drivers of the speeding juggernauts but also, by increasing the public's interest in motor cars, to auto manufacturers whose business increased. Louis Chevrolet demonstrated great skill at handling fast cars and his name was soon as familiar to racing fans as Barney Oldfield's, one of the greatest of that era. Louis's success was due almost as much to his mechanical ability in tuning his racer as to his driving skill.

It was through his racing triumphs that Louis Chevrolet became associated with W. C. Durant. An aggressive businessman, Durant was to make a name for himself in the growing auto industry as founder of the General Motors Corporation. In time, this concern was to grow into one of the world's largest motor car manufacturers. Durant persuaded Chevrolet to give up the dangerous sport of racing cars and, instead, to design and build automobiles for the public. Louis was about ready to quit racing and agreed to join forces with Durant. Because of his wide racing popularity, Louis's name was given to the new auto enterprise, the Chevrolet Company. It began business in 1912. Louis Chevrolet became its chief designer.

The first car produced by the Chevrolet Company was a six-cylinder model that sold at the factory for slightly more than $2000. This was a lot of money in those days and sales were poor. Realizing that a lower-priced car might sell better, Chevrolet came out with a four-cylinder model called the Baby Grand. It had a price tag of $875 and sold much better than the company's first model. But Chevrolet's earliest and biggest success came with the "490" car. It was almost identical to the Baby Grand except in price, which was $490. This brought the Chevrolet within reach of many more potential car buyers and soon large numbers of them were rolling along city streets and country roads.

The Chevrolet Company produced many successful car models, not the least of which was the Royal Mail Roadster made in 1914. The 1915 version of this car, practically the same as its predecessor, is the one to be built as a model. The real motor car was a sturdy vehicle that served its owners well. The distinctive oval fuel tank to the rear of the driver's seat was a common feature on many cars of that era. The toolbox on the tail end of the roadster was a must on all early automobiles.

The Chevrolet Company continued in business as an independent auto manufacturer for five years. In the hectic years just before and after World War I, a number of motor car manufacturers, including the Chevrolet Company, failed financially or were taken over by others. In 1917, the Chevrolet Company was absorbed by the General Motors Corporation.

BUILDING THE 1915 CHEVROLET

Chassis (Diagram 1)
The chassis is made from rigid cardboard. Draw and cut out this piece as shown in Diagram 1. Paint the chassis yellow or any color you wish. Just remember that whatever color you choose will be the main color of your car model.

Radiator (Diagram 2)
The first unit to be made and attached to the chassis is the motor compartment. It consists of three pieces: the radiator, the rear wall, and the motor hood. All are made the same color as the chassis.

The radiator or front end is made first. Draw and cut out this piece from construction paper as shown in Diagram 2. While the radiator is still flat on your work surface, draw the grill lines on one side for the radiator front as shown in Diagram 2. Use black crayon if you wish, but pen and black drawing ink make a much

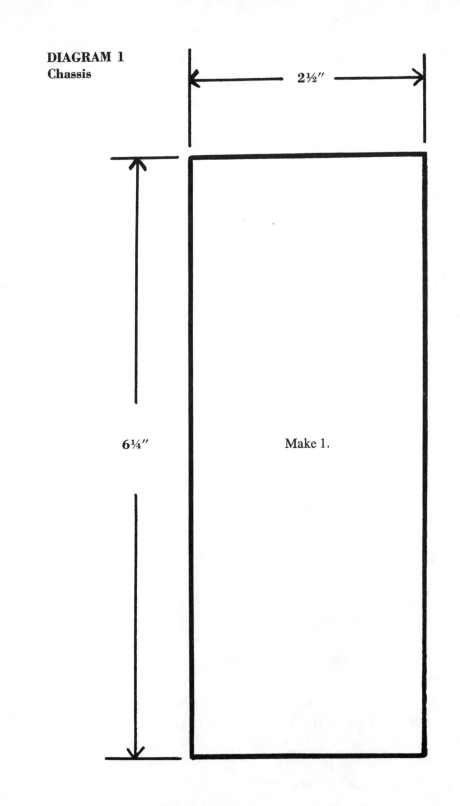

DIAGRAM 1
Chassis

2½″

6¼″

Make 1.

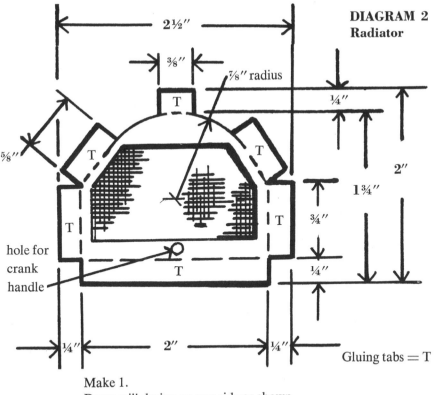

DIAGRAM 2
Radiator

2½″

⅜″

⅞″ radius

¼″

⅝″

2″

1¾″

¾″

¼″

hole for
crank
handle

T

¼″

2″

¼″

Gluing tabs = T

Make 1.
Draw grill design on one side as shown.

neater-looking grill. When the grill design is finished, make a hole with a sharp-pointed nail in the bottom portion of the radiator as shown in Diagram 2. The hole is for the crank handle and should be just big enough for a round toothpick to slip through.

Bend along the dotted lines, making the gluing tab folds as straight as possible. Glue the bottom tab to the front edge of the chassis so the radiator is ¼ inch from the edge. Make sure that the radiator is parallel to the front edge and the same distance from both sides of the chassis.

Rear Wall of Motor Compartment (Diagram 3)

The rear wall or back end of the motor compartment is made from rigid cardboard. Draw and cut out this piece as shown in Diagram 3. You may paint this part if you wish, but it is not necessary since

DIAGRAM 3
Rear Wall of Motor Compartment

Make 1.

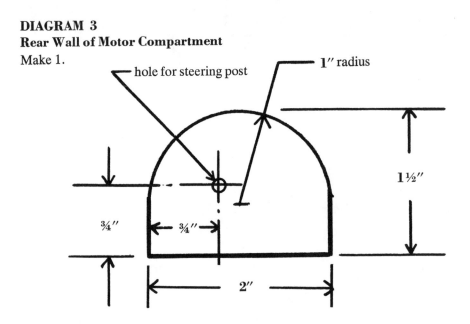

hole for steering post

1″ radius

1½″

¾″   ¾″

2″

the rear wall will be almost completely hidden by other sections of the model.

Make the hole for the steering post as shown in Diagram 3, using a nail or other sharp-pointed tool to start the hole. With the point of your pencil, enlarge it just enough for a large match-stick to fit through.

Glue the rear wall to the chassis so it is 1⅞ inches from the radiator and ¼ inch from each side of the chassis. Be sure to attach this piece accurately or your motor compartment covering may end up looking slightly crooked.

Motor Hood (Diagram 4)

The motor hood or covering is a simple shape, but it has considerable design work on it. Draw and cut out this piece from construction paper as shown in Diagram 4. Draw the design work shown in Diagram 4 as neatly as you can. Use black crayon if you like, or pen and black drawing ink.

The motor hood forms the curved sides and top of the motor

138

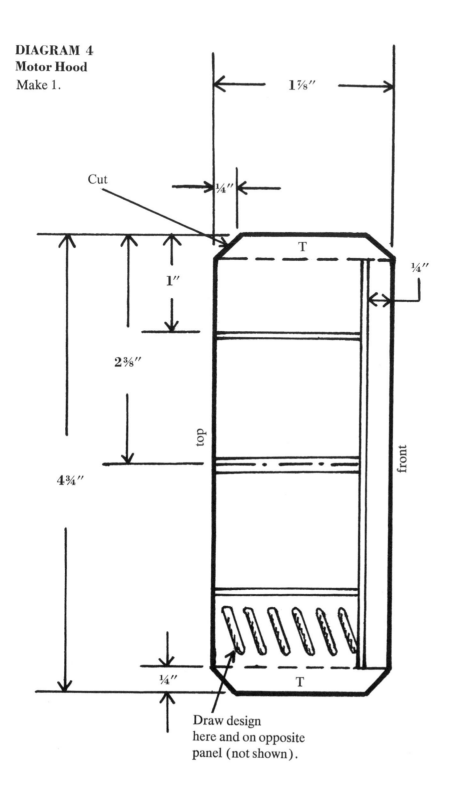

DIAGRAM 4
Motor Hood
Make 1.

1⅞″

Cut

¼″

T

¼″

1″

2⅜″

top

front

4¾″

T

¼″

Draw design
here and on opposite
panel (not shown).

compartment. With the design side outward, attach one of its gluing tabs to the side of the chassis between the radiator and the rear wall of the motor compartment. Be sure the fold edge is ¼ inch from the edge of the chassis. Now attach the motor hood to the radiator gluing tabs, one tab at a time. Make certain that the front edge of the motor hood is even with the outer edge of the radiator. Put a generous amount of glue on the radiator tabs and let them dry for a few minutes before pressing them in place. The two pieces will stick together better and faster this way. Glue the back end of the motor hood to the rear wall as you proceed around the radiator edge. Put a generous amount of glue along the edge of the rear wall, let it dry, then press the back edge of the hood to it. Run your finger over the attachment several times to make sure the hood and rear wall are firmly glued.

The second gluing tab of the motor hood is the last to be attached. For this tab, put the glue along the chassis edge where the attachment is to be made. Tuck the tab inside the motor compartment, being careful to keep its fold edge ¼ inch from the chassis edge. This completes the motor compartment.

Cowling Support and Gauges (Diagram 5)

The cowling support is part of the frame for the forward part of the body between the motor compartment and the driver's section. The upper part of the cowling support facing the driver's section also serves as a dashboard.

Draw and cut out the cowling support from rigid cardboard as shown in Diagram 5. Paint the support with yellow poster paint, or whatever color you have chosen for your model.

Draw and cut out dashboard gauges #1, #2, and #3 from black construction paper as shown in Diagram 5. Glue the gauges to the cowling support as indicated in Diagram 5.

Once the gauges are firmly in place, the cowling support can be attached to the chassis. On each side of the chassis, measure and mark a point ¾ inch from the rear of the motor compartment. Draw a light pencil line connecting these two points. Glue

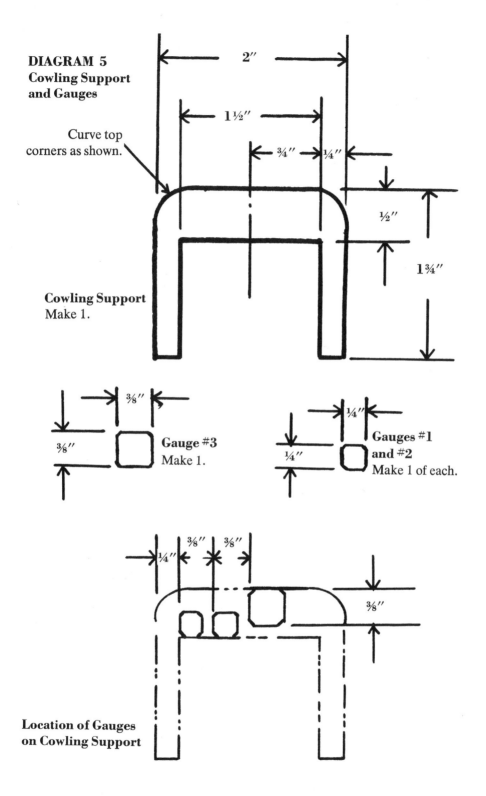

**DIAGRAM 5
Cowling Support
and Gauges**

Curve top
corners as shown.

2″

1½″

¾″ ¼″

½″

1¾″

Cowling Support
Make 1.

⅜″

⅜″

Gauge #3
Make 1.

¼″

¼″

**Gauges #1
and #2**
Make 1 of each.

¼″ ⅜″ ⅜″

⅜″

**Location of Gauges
on Cowling Support**

the ends of the cowling support's legs to the chassis ¼ inch in from each side; use the pencil line as a guide for keeping the support parallel to the motor compartment. The cowling support attachment may seem weak now but it will become a good deal stronger after the cowl coverings are glued in place.

Slanted Footboard (Diagram 6)

Before attaching the cowl coverings, it is convenient to install the slanted footboard. Draw and cut out this part from rigid cardboard as shown in Diagram 6. Paint the footboard black, using poster paint. Mark the attachment points for the brake, clutch, and gas pedals as shown in Diagram 6, using yellow crayon or pencil. Glue the footboard in place at an angle so that one long edge rests against the rear wall of the motor compartment and the other is attached to the chassis along the pencil line between the legs of the cowling support.

Floor Mat (Diagram 7)

This is also a good time to glue the floor mat in place. Draw and cut out this piece from black construction paper as shown in Diagram 7. Glue it flat to the chassis so that one long side is even with the legs of the cowling support. The area in which the floor mat is glued will later be called the driver's compartment.

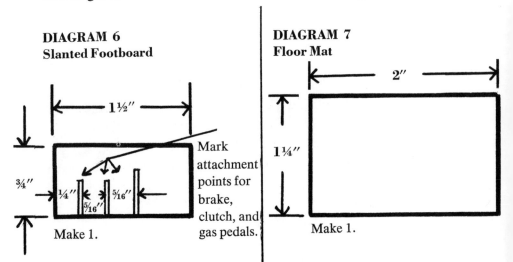

DIAGRAM 6
Slanted Footboard

Mark attachment points for brake, clutch, and gas pedals.

Make 1.

DIAGRAM 7
Floor Mat

Make 1.

Cowl Coverings #1 and #2 (Diagram 8)

The cowl coverings partly enclose the driver's section. Fitting and gluing these pieces are the hardest tasks in constructing this Chevrolet model. This is because the coverings have to be formed and glued around curves that bend in two or more directions. However, if you work slowly and carefully and have the patience of a true model-maker, you will have little difficulty attaching these pieces.

Draw and cut out the single piece for cowl coverings #1 and #2 as shown in Diagram 8. Use the color construction paper you have chosen for your model. Draw the design for the two doors on one side as shown in the diagram. Use black crayon if you wish, but pen and black drawing ink will produce better results.

When you have finished the design, cut the piece in half, as indicated in Diagram 8, to form the two separate cowl coverings. Then cut the ½-inch slits in the front edge of each covering. These slits will help eliminate bulges in the coverings as you shape and glue them over the cowling support and motor compartment. Cutting the cowl coverings into two separate parts also makes it easier to glue them in place.

The cowl coverings have no gluing tabs. Instead, glue their forward sections directly to the edges of the motor compartment and cowling support. Keep running your finger over the connecting edge of the coverings until they are firmly attached. The door portion of the cowl coverings is not glued until other parts of the model have been added.

Cowl Covering #3 (Diagram 8)

Cowl covering #3 completes the enclosure of the forward part of the model. Draw and cut out this piece as shown in Diagram 8. Use the same color construction paper you used for coverings #1 and #2. Bend the panel so it covers the remaining space between the top of the motor compartment and the cowling support. Glue all four edges in place. Trim away any overhang along the top of the dashboard with your scissors or knife.

DIAGRAM 8
Cowl Coverings

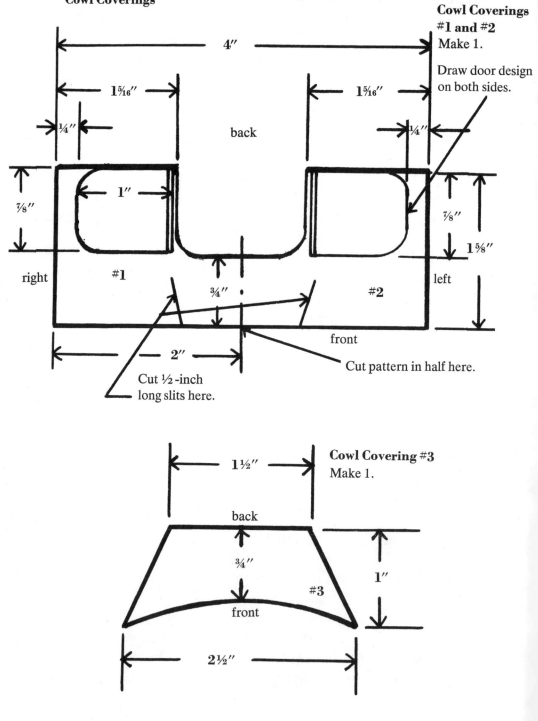

Cowl Coverings #1 and #2
Make 1.

Draw door design on both sides.

4″

1⁵⁄₁₆″   1⁵⁄₁₆″

¼″   ¼″

back

1″

⅞″

right   #1

#2   left

¾″

2″

front

Cut pattern in half here.

Cut ½-inch long slits here.

⅞″

1⅝″

Cowl Covering #3
Make 1.

1½″

back

¾″

#3   1″

front

2½″

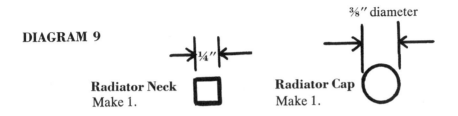

DIAGRAM 9

⅜" diameter

¼"

Radiator Neck
Make 1.

Radiator Cap
Make 1.

Radiator Neck and Cap (Diagram 9)

After wrestling with the cowl coverings, making and installing the radiator neck and cap will seem extremely easy. Cut the neck from a drinking straw to the length shown in Diagram 9. Paint this part the color you have chosen for your model.

Cut the radiator cap from black construction paper as shown in Diagram 9. Since this is such a small piece, you may find cuticle scissors more convenient than larger scissors for cutting the disc.

Glue the cap to one end of the neck. Then glue the completed unit to the forward end of the top of the radiator. See the photograph of the finished model on page 133.

Seat Base (Diagram 10)

On the early cars, seats for the drivers and passengers were extremely high. There was no problem seeing the road ahead. The seat base on this Chevrolet model helped give the driver a lofty perch.

Draw and cut out the seat base as shown in Diagram 10. Use construction paper in the color you have chosen for your model. Fold along the dotted lines with extreme care. The seat base must fit square and level on the chassis or the driver's seat will be crooked.

The seat base is attached to the chassis on three of its sides, with the front panel edge to edge with the floor mat. Glue one tab at a time to the chassis, beginning with either long side attachment. The fold edge of the tab should be even with the chassis. The narrow forward strip extends beneath the door of the cowl covering. Next glue the short front tab in place, and then attach the remaining side tab. Finally, glue the two forward side strips to the cowl coverings.

DIAGRAM 10
Seat Base
Make 1.

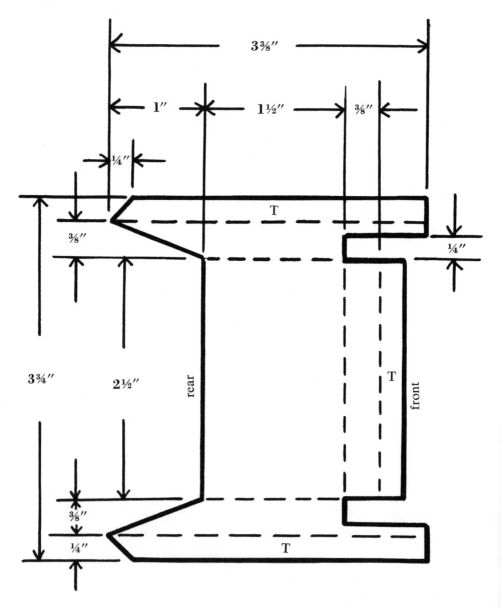

Seat Sides (Diagram 11)

Once the seat base is firmly attached, the seat proper can be installed. It consists of two flat sides and back with cushions, and a raised seat cushion.

Begin with the two sides. Draw and cut out these pieces as shown in Diagram 11. Use the color construction paper you have chosen for your model. Draw the black border with pen and ink or black crayon on one side of each piece. Remember to do this on opposite sides for the right and left pieces. Bend the gluing tabs toward the undecorated side of each piece.

Side Cushions (Diagram 11)

Before the sides of the seat can be glued in place, cushions must be added to their inner surface. Draw and cut out the cushions as shown in Diagram 11, using light green construction paper. You may, if you wish, use the pattern for the seat sides to make the cushion pieces, since their shapes are identical except for the seat sides' gluing tabs. Draw the design as shown in the diagram on one side of each cushion, using pen and black ink. Glue one cushion to the plain surface of each side piece. When the cushions and seat sides are firmly attached, trim away any overhang with your scissors.

Place the seat sides on top of the seat base, cushion sides facing inward. Keep the folds of the bottom gluing tabs even with the edges of the seat base sides. Also keep the forward corners of the seat sides even with the forward corners of the seat base. Glue the tabs in place. The sides will be wobbly, of course, until they are attached to the seat back.

Seat Back (Diagram 12)

Draw and cut out the back of the seat as shown in Diagram 12. Use the same color construction paper you used for the sides. Fold the gluing tab carefully, and set the piece aside until you have made its cushion.

DIAGRAM 11

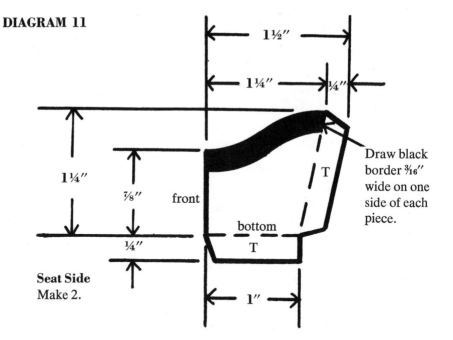

1½″

1¼″

¼″

1¼″

⅞″

front

bottom

T

T

¼″

1″

Draw black border ³⁄₁₆″ wide on one side of each piece.

Seat Side
Make 2.

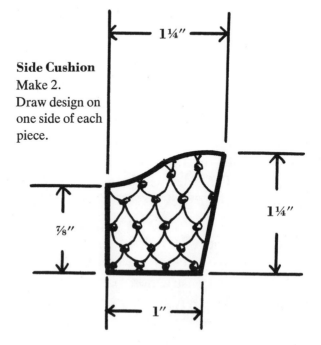

1¼″

Side Cushion
Make 2.
Draw design on one side of each piece.

⅞″

1¼″

1″

Back Cushion (Diagram 12)

The cushion for the seat back is exactly like the seat back without a gluing tab. Draw and cut out the cushion from light green construction paper as shown in Diagram 12. (Again, you may trace the pattern for the seat back instead, omitting the gluing tab.) Draw the cushion design on one side, using pen and black ink. Glue the completed cushion pattern to the gluing tab side of the seat back. Trim any overhang of the two glued parts with your scissors.

DIAGRAM 12

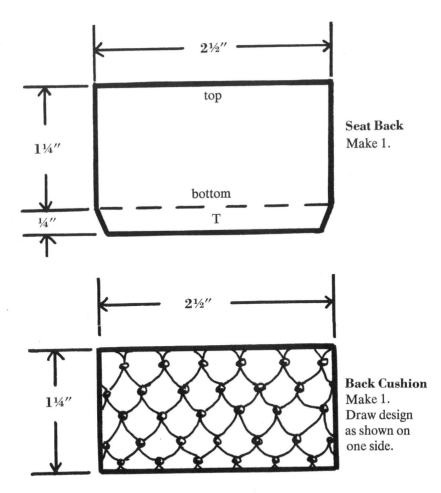

2½″

1¼″

¼″

top

bottom

T

Seat Back
Make 1.

2½″

1¼″

Back Cushion
Make 1.
Draw design
as shown on
one side.

Place the seat back, cushion side facing forward, on top of the seat base. Glue the bottom gluing tab to the seat base first so that the fold edge and bottom corners are even with the back edge of the seat base. Then glue the tabs extending from the seat sides to the back of the seat back. Try to keep the corners formed by the back and sides perfectly square.

Seat Cushion (Diagram 13)

Unlike the seat sides and back, the seat cushion is made as a single piece. Draw and cut out the seat cushion as shown in Diagram 13,

DIAGRAM 13
Seat Cushion
Make 1.
Draw design
as shown on one side.

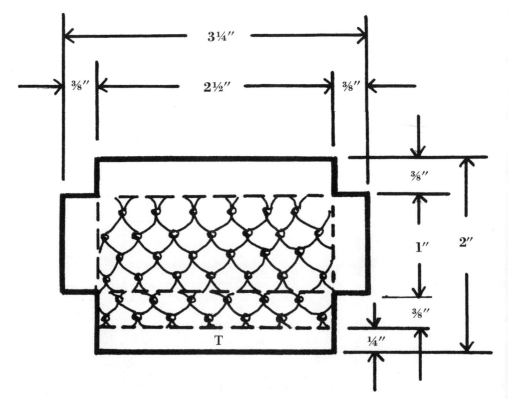

using light green construction paper. Draw the cushion design on one side as shown with pen and black drawing ink. Fold along the dotted lines toward the plain side of the piece, forming a box-like shape that is open at the bottom. It is important to do this carefully so that the seat cushion will fit between the seat sides. Slide the seat cushion in place, with the narrow decorated panel facing forward, to make sure it fits properly. The forward sections of the seat cushion and seat base should be even. Glue the front gluing tab of the cushion to the front edge of the seat base. Then glue the sides and back of the seat cushion to the inner sides and back of the seat. Once the seat cushion is in place, the entire driver's compartment will be quite strong.

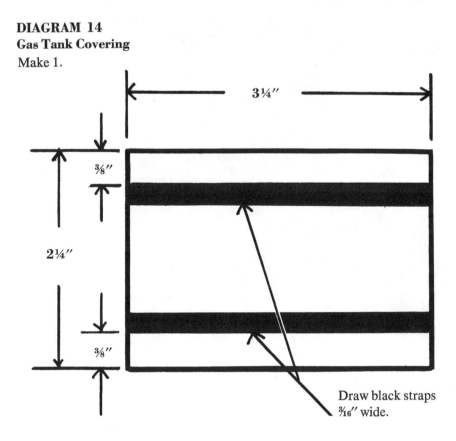

DIAGRAM 14
Gas Tank Covering
Make 1.

3¼″

⅜″

2¼″

⅜″

Draw black straps
³⁄₁₆″ wide.

Gas Tank Covering (Diagram 14)

On early cars, no attempt was made to hide the fuel tank. This came with more modern automobile design. The Chevrolet you are making as a model had its gas tank directly behind the driver's seat.

Draw and cut out the tank covering as shown in Diagram 14. Use the same color construction paper you used for the motor compartment and cowl coverings. Draw the black straps on one side of the pattern with pen and black drawing ink. To help form the oval shape of the tank covering, draw the plain side of the pattern lengthwise over the edge of your work surface or ruler. Repeat this several times until the paper begins to curl. Set the covering aside until the ends have been made.

152

Gas Tank Ends (Diagram 15)

The two ends of the gas tank are oval shapes. Draw and cut out these pieces as shown in Diagram 15, using the same color construction paper you used for the covering. Fold along the dotted lines carefully, bending the tabs in opposite directions for the right and left ends.

The ends are connected to one another by a rigid cardboard stiffener, which also makes it easier to assemble the tank and serves as a support for the finished piece. Draw and cut out the stiffener as shown in Diagram 15. Glue the ends to the stiffener as shown in Assembly Diagram 15. Make sure that the ends face one another exactly, and that the gluing tabs are on the inside.

DIAGRAM 15

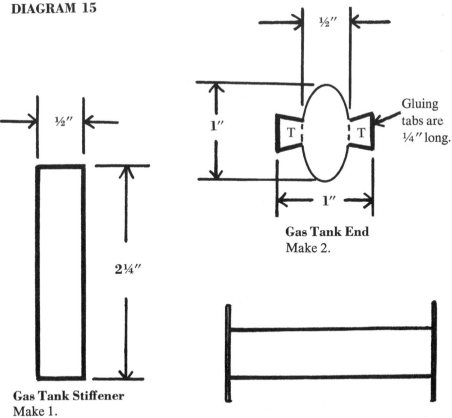

½″

1″

1″

Gluing tabs are ¼″ long.

Gas Tank End
Make 2.

½″

2¼″

Gas Tank Stiffener
Make 1.

Gas Tank Ends-Stiffener Assembly

Now you are ready to glue the covering to the ends of the gas tank. This takes a little patience. Place the long sides of the covering edge to edge with the ends so that one short covering side rests on top of one pair of gluing tabs. Glue in place. Put a generous amount of glue on the edge of the ends, and gradually work around the oval shapes, pressing the covering to both edges at the same time. Attach the second pair of gluing tabs as you reach them. When you return to your starting point, overlap the ends of the covering and glue firmly together.

Gas Tank Filler Neck and Cap (Diagram 16)

The last parts to be attached to the gas tank are the filler neck and cap. Cut the neck from a drinking straw to the length given in Diagram 16. Paint the neck with black poster paint.

Cut the disc-shaped cap to the size shown in Diagram 16. Use the same color construction paper you used for the tank covering. Glue the disc so that it is centered on one open end of the neck. Now glue this unit to the center of either narrow side of the tank. See Assembly Diagram 16.

Place the completed gas tank directly behind the driver's seat at a slight angle. See the photograph of the finished model on page 186. Rest the overlapped covering ends against the seat back, and glue this part of the tank to the seat back.

DIAGRAM 16

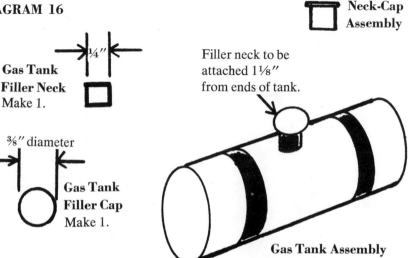

Neck-Cap
Assembly

**Gas Tank
Filler Neck
Make 1.**

¼″

Filler neck to be
attached 1⅛″
from ends of tank.

⅜″ diameter

**Gas Tank
Filler Cap
Make 1.**

Gas Tank Assembly

DIAGRAM 17
Toolbox
Make 1.

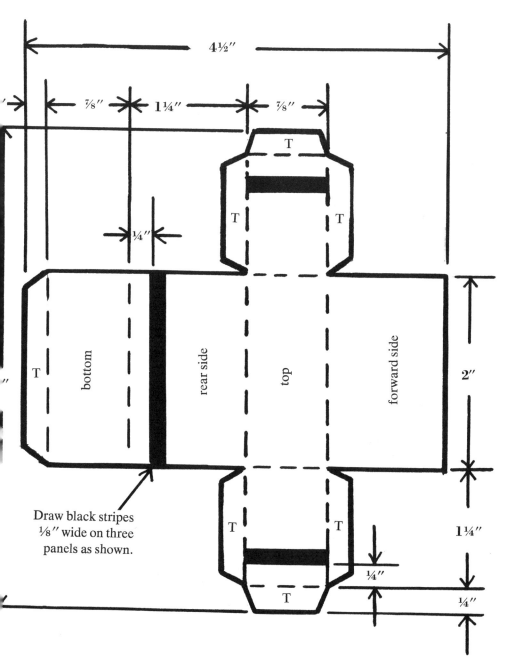

4½″

⅞″ 1¼″ ⅞″

¼″

T

T T

T bottom rear side top forward side 2″

T T

¼″ 1¼″

Draw black stripes
⅛″ wide on three
panels as shown.

T

¼″

Toolbox (Diagram 17)

In the early days of the automobile, no driver would be without a big box of tools and essential spare parts. You never knew when the engine of your car would quit and you would have to get out and tinker with it to get it running again. The toolbox on this Chevrolet was a generous-sized unit.

Draw and cut out this piece as shown in Diagram 17. Use brown construction paper to make it look like wood. Draw the black stripes on one side of the three outside panels, as shown in Diagram 17, using pen and black drawing ink. Score along the dotted lines carefully, and fold and glue the unit into a boxlike shape. Glue the toolbox to the back end of the chassis with the stripes near the bottom and the plain side resting against the gas tank. See the photograph of the finished model on page 186.

Brake and Clutch Pedals (Diagram 18)

Before installing the roof of the model, making access to the driver's section a bit more difficult, it is a good idea to add the remaining small parts to the driver's compartment. Begin with the brake and clutch pedals. Draw and cut out these parts as shown in Diagram 18. Use rigid cardboard and paint the pedals the color you have chosen for your model.

These small parts are glued partly to the slanted footboard and partly to the floor mat. See Diagram 18 for their location. Glue both pedals to the floor mat along their slanted edges and to the footboard along the adjacent ¼-inch edges. The longest pedal edges face the driver. Since the brake and clutch parts are rather small, tweezers might make it easier to handle these pieces. Be sure to let the glue dry for a few minutes and become tacky before pressing the pedals in place. This will make them hold in position faster.

Gas Pedal (Diagram 18)

The gas pedal is a slightly larger version of the brake and clutch pedals. Draw and cut out this piece from rigid cardboard as shown in Diagram 18. Paint it the same color as the other foot pedals. Hold it with tweezers while you glue it to the footboard and floor mat. The slanted edge is glued to the floor mat and the adjacent ⅜-inch edge is glued to the footboard. The longest edge faces the driver. Again, let the glue dry for a few minutes and become tacky before pressing the pedal in place.

DIAGRAM 18
Foot Pedals

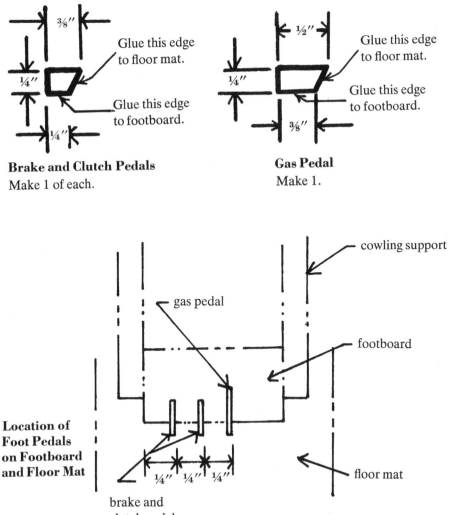

⅜″
¼″
¼″

Glue this edge to floor mat.

Glue this edge to footboard.

Brake and Clutch Pedals
Make 1 of each.

½″
¼″
⅜″

Glue this edge to floor mat.

Glue this edge to footboard.

Gas Pedal
Make 1.

cowling support

gas pedal

footboard

Location of Foot Pedals on Footboard and Floor Mat

¼″ ¼″ ¼″

brake and clutch pedals

floor mat

Hand Brake (Diagram 19)

The hand brake consists of a handle and grip. The handle is made from round toothpick wood. Cut the toothpick to the length shown in Diagram 19. Paint it the same color as the foot pedals.

A hand grip is attached to the upper part of the hand brake handle. Cut the hand grip from round toothpick wood to the length given in Diagram 19. Paint this part blue. Glue it to the upper end of the handle as shown in Assembly Diagram 19.

DIAGRAM 19

Hand Brake Handle
Make 1.

Hand Brake Grip
Make 1.

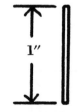

Gear Shift Handle
Make 1.

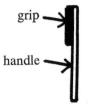

Hand Brake Assembly

Gear Shift Assembly

Gear Shift Knob
Make 1.

Gear Shift (Diagram 19)

The gear shift handle is also made from round toothpick wood. Cut the handle to the length given in Diagram 19 and paint it the same color as the hand brake handle.

On the top end of the gear shift handle is a small shift knob. Cut the knob from round toothpick wood to the length shown in Diagram 19. Paint the knob black. When it is dry, glue the knob to the end of the gear shift handle as shown in Assembly Diagram 19.

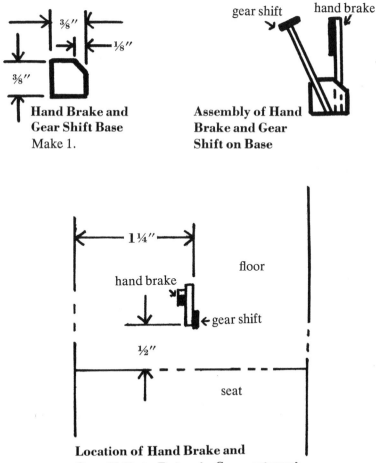

⅜″

⅛″

⅜″

**Hand Brake and
Gear Shift Base**
Make 1.

gear shift　　hand brake

**Assembly of Hand
Brake and Gear
Shift on Base**

1¼″

floor

hand brake

gear shift

½″

seat

**Location of Hand Brake and
Gear Shift in Driver's Compartment**

Hand Brake and Gear Shift Base (Diagram 19)

Both the hand brake and gear shift are glued to a base which, in turn, is glued to the floor mat of the driver's compartment. The base is a small square with one corner lopped off.

Draw and cut out this piece as shown in Diagram 19, using rigid cardboard. Paint the base the same color as the hand brake and gear shift handles. When it is dry, glue the hand brake and gear shift to it on opposite sides and in the positions shown in Assembly Diagram 19.

After the hand brake and gear shift have been firmly glued to the base, attach the unit to the floor of the driver's compartment. Position it parallel to and the same distance from the right and left sides of the driver's compartment, and ½ inch in front of the seat base. See Diagram 19.

Steering Unit (Diagram 20)

The steering unit consists of a post and wheel. It is the last item to be added to the driver's compartment.

Cut the steering post from large matchstick wood to the length shown in Diagram 20, cutting one end at an angle. Paint the post the same color as the foot pedals.

Cut the steering wheel from rigid cardboard as shown in Diagram 20. Try to select cardboard that is not too thick to make your circle-cutting easier. Draw the spokes and rim on both sides of the wheel as shown in Diagram 20. Use either black crayon or pen and black drawing ink.

Lay the finished wheel flat on your work surface and put a generous amount of glue on its center point. Let the glue dry for a few minutes and become tacky. Press the square end of the steering post onto the glued center. Hold the post upright for a few minutes to make sure it will stand by itself. Before the glue has thoroughly hardened, stand your ruler on end near the post to check the post's perpendicular position. Turn the wheel slowly and make sure the post is perfectly upright all around the circle.

160

DIAGRAM 20
Steering Unit

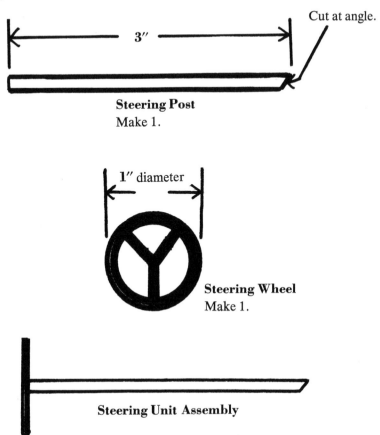

Cut at angle.

3″

Steering Post
Make 1.

1″ diameter

Steering Wheel
Make 1.

Steering Unit Assembly

When the wheel and post are firmly attached, the steering unit can be installed through the hole in the rear wall of the motor compartment. Put a generous amount of glue on the slanted end of the post and slide it through the hole at an angle. Continue pushing the post through the hole until it touches the chassis floor inside the motor compartment. Hold it briefly to make sure it is securely glued. The wheel end of the steering unit should be just above the edge of the driver's seat. To reinforce the steering post, put a generous amount of glue at the point where it enters the motor compartment wall.

DIAGRAM 21
Windshield
Make 1.

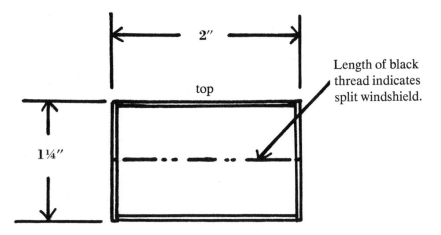

Windshield (Diagram 21)

The windshield on this model is a simple frame made from round toothpicks. Cut the wood to the lengths given in Diagram 21. Assemble the pieces on your flat work surface and glue the four corners. When the glue is almost dry, pry the frame loose from the work surface by sliding the flat side of your knife under each glued joint. Before the pieces are permanently attached, look at the frame sideways to make sure it is still perfectly square. Then put it aside to allow the glue to thoroughly harden.

When the glue is completely dry, tie a length of black thread across the windshield at the center of the short sides. This gives the windshield the appearance of being split into two halves.

Glue the completed windshield along one side to the top edge of the cowling support. See the photograph of the finished model on page 133. Put a generous amount of glue along the edge and allow the glue to dry and become tacky. Press the windshield in place, and hold briefly until it stands alone in a perpendicular position.

Side Frames of Roof (Diagrams 22-23)

The roof frame for this model consists of two side frames connected at the top by three crosspieces. Make the two side frames
first, one at a time.

With black crayon or a soft lead pencil, draw the pattern for
the side frame, as shown in Diagram 22, on a smooth, flat piece of
wood or shiny rigid cardboard. See Diagram 23 for the length of
each numbered piece. Except for length #1, which is cut from
matchstick wood, all the pieces are cut from round toothpicks.
Cut the pieces and lay them on their corresponding numbers on
the pattern. Put a generous amount of glue on all the connecting
points, and let the glue dry for about half an hour. Then use the

DIAGRAM 22
Side Frames of Roof
Make 2.

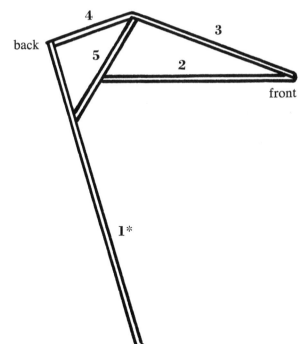

See Diagram 23 for length of each piece.
Asterisk indicates matchstick wood.

DIAGRAM 23
Lengths of Roof Frame Parts

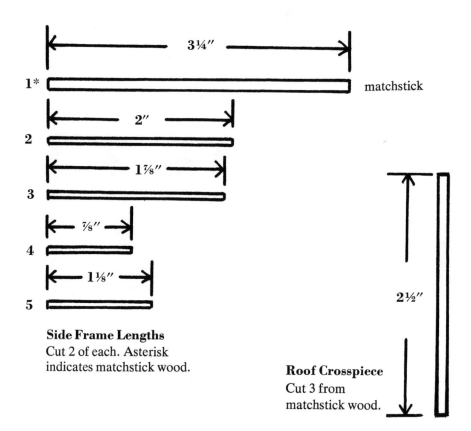

Side Frame Lengths
Cut 2 of each. Asterisk
indicates matchstick wood.

Roof Crosspiece
Cut 3 from
matchstick wood.

flat side of your knife and slide it under each glued joint, prying them free of your work surface. While the pieces are still movable, look at the frame sideways to make sure all the pieces are in a straight line. Set this frame aside to let the glue harden permanently while you work on the second frame.

Roof Crosspieces (Diagram 23)
Once both side frames are securely glued, they can be joined together by the three crosspieces. Cut these three pieces from large matchstick wood to the length given in Diagram 23.

Roof Frame Assembly (Diagram 24)

An easy way to attach the crosspieces to the side frames is to work with the parts in an upside down position. Lay two of the cross-pieces on your work surface, and put a generous amount of glue on their ends. Then place the side frames upside down on the glued ends at joints B-B and C-C. Put jars of poster paint, or other small objects, against the frames to hold them at perfect right angles to the crosspieces until the glue dries. Once these two cross-pieces are firmly attached, glue the remaining front crosspiece in place at joint A-A. For this piece, you might find it easier to work

DIAGRAM 24
Roof Frame Assembly

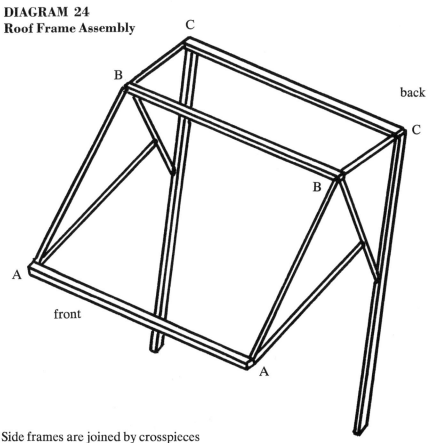

Side frames are joined by crosspieces
at joints A-A, B-B, and C-C.

with the frame in a right side up position. See Assembly Diagram 24.

When the roof frame is thoroughly dry, paint the entire unit black. Use poster paint or black drawing ink. Set the painted frame aside to dry while you make the roof covering.

DIAGRAM 25
Side Roof Panels
Make 2.

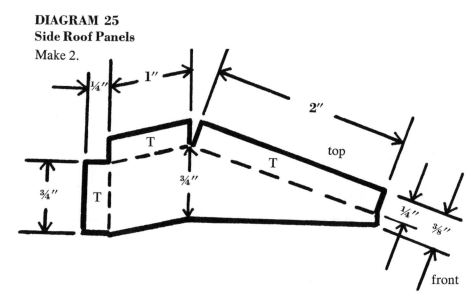

Side Roof Panels (Diagram 25)

The roof covering is made in four parts: two side panels, one top, and one back. The side panels are made and attached first.

Draw and cut out the side roof panels from black construction paper as shown in Diagram 25. Lightly score along the dotted lines, being careful just to crease and not to cut the gluing tabs. Remember that the gluing tabs on the right and left panels fold in opposite directions.

Place the panels on the roof frame to make sure they fit properly. Do not be alarmed by the width of the top gluing tabs. They will later serve as attachment points for the top roof panel. Make certain that the long, bottom edge of each panel covers and is horizontal to length #2 of the side frames. Glue the side panels to the roof frame wherever they touch the wood structure.

166

Top Roof Panel (Diagram 26)

Draw and cut out the rectangular roof top from black construction paper as shown in Diagram 26. Lightly score along the dotted lines of the gluing tabs and the crosswise crease. Place the roof top on the frame to make sure it fits correctly. Trim any overhang with your scissors. Glue the roof top to the gluing tabs of the side panels and to the front and rear crosspieces.

DIAGRAM 26
Top Roof Panel

Make 1.

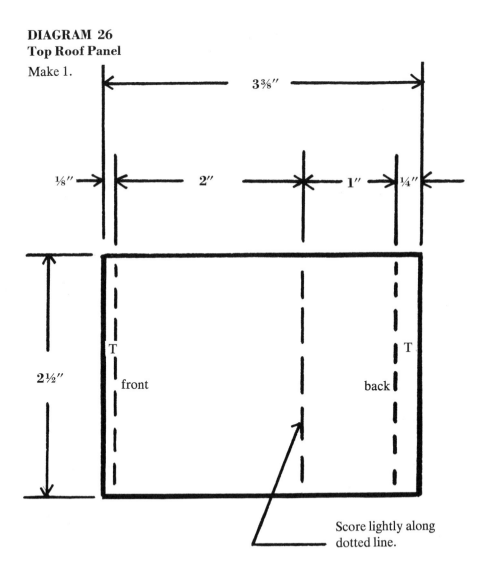

$3\frac{3}{8}''$

$\frac{1}{8}''$ $2''$ $1''$ $\frac{1}{4}''$

$2\frac{1}{2}''$

T   front   back   T

Score lightly along dotted line.

DIAGRAM 27
Back Roof Panel
Make 1.

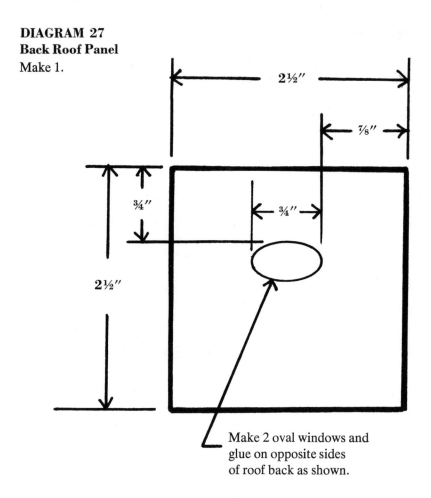

Make 2 oval windows and
glue on opposite sides
of roof back as shown.

Back Roof Panel (Diagram 27)

Draw and cut out the square roof back from black construction
paper as shown in Diagram 27. Then draw and cut out the two
oval windows from white construction paper as shown in Diagram 27. Glue one window to each side of the roof back, following the measurements shown in Diagram 27.

Glue the top edge of the roof back directly to the rear gluing
tab of the roof top. The bottom edge of the back will be glued to
the back of the driver's seat after the roof unit has been attached
to the model.

168

Installing the Roof

Place the roof unit over the driver's compartment so that the ends of the side frame supports are at the forward corners of the seat cushion, and the front crosspiece rests on the top edge of the windshield. Glue the lower part of the side frame supports to the sides of the seat, using metal spring-type hair clips to hold the supports in place until the glue dries. Then glue the front crosspiece to the top edge of the windshield, again holding the two parts together with clips until they are firmly attached. Finally, glue the lower edge of the roof back to the back of the driver's seat. The roof back forms a gentle rearward slope from the seat back to the top of the roof. See the photograph of the finished model on page 186. This completes the construction and installation of the roof unit.

DIAGRAM 28
Back Splashes
Make 2.

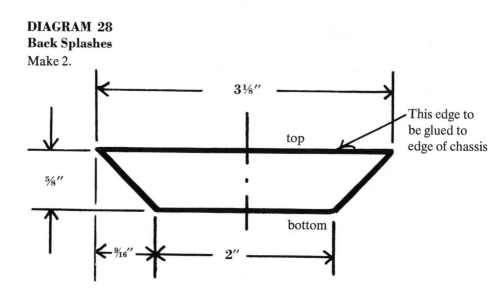

Back Splashes (Diagram 28)

A back splash on each side of the real Chevrolet prevented stones and mud from flying up onto the running board. Draw and cut out these pieces from rigid cardboard as shown in Diagram 28. Paint them the color you have chosen for your model.

Turn the car model upside down and place the long side of one back splash on the underside of the chassis along either side edge. The forward point of the back splash should be 1⅞ inches from the front edge of the chassis. Glue the back splash to the chassis so that the two parts are at right angles to one another. Glue the second back splash to the opposite side in the same way.

DIAGRAM 29
Running Boards

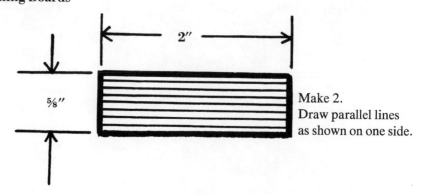

Running Boards (Diagram 29)

Draw and cut out the two running boards from rigid cardboard as shown in Diagram 29. Draw the parallel lines with pen and black drawing ink as shown on one side of each piece. One running board is attached to each back splash at perfect right angles. Glue the running boards in place along either long side.

Wheels (Diagram 30)

Draw and cut out the four wheels from rigid cardboard as shown in Diagram 30. Try to find cardboard that is not too thick so you can cut the circles easily. Draw the wheel design on both sides of each wheel. Use black crayon if you wish, but pen and black drawing ink are better.

Wheel Boxes (Diagram 30)

A wheel box, glued to the center of each wheel, connects the wheel to the axle. Draw and cut out these four pieces from black construction paper as shown in Diagram 30. Carefully cut the four corner slits as shown, as well as the "X" in the center. The center slots should be just wide enough for a matchstick to slide through. If they are too wide, the axles will not fit firmly no matter how much glue you add. Fold along the dotted lines to form boxlike shapes which are open at the bottom. Make sure the wheel boxes are folded accurately, or the wheel-axle connections on your finished model will be crooked. Glue the boxes together at the corner gluing tabs.

Glue one wheel box, "X" side facing outward, to the exact center of one side of each wheel. This side of the wheel is now the inner or axle side.

Axles (Diagram 30)

The two axles for the Chevrolet model are made from large matchstick wood. Cut these to the length shown in Diagram 30. Paint them the color you have chosen for your model.

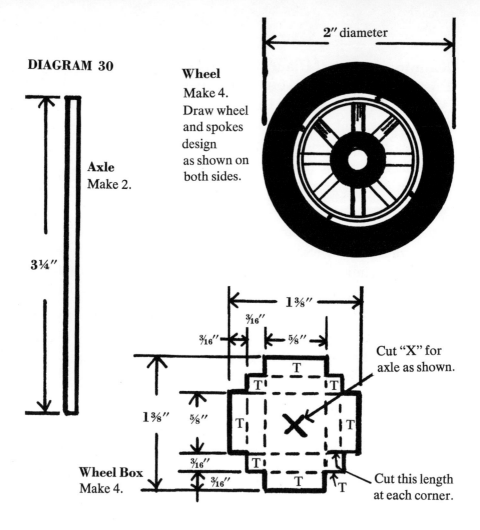

DIAGRAM 30

Axle
Make 2.

3¼″

2″ diameter

Wheel
Make 4.
Draw wheel
and spokes
design
as shown on
both sides.

1⅜″

³⁄₁₆″

³⁄₁₆″   ⅝″

Cut "X" for
axle as shown.

T

T   T

1⅜″   ⅝″   T   ✕   T

³⁄₁₆″   T

Wheel Box
Make 4.

³⁄₁₆″   T   T

Cut this length
at each corner.

Lay one of the wheels flat on your work surface. Put a generous amount of glue on one of the axle ends, and push it through the "X" of the wheel box. Make sure the axle forms a perfect right angle with the wheel. Check its position by holding your ruler upright near the axle and turning the wheel slowly around. Repeat this procedure for the second axle. The second set of wheels will be attached later. Set the wheel-axle units aside to let the glue permanently harden while you make the leaf spring units.

Leaf Springs (Diagram 31)

There are four leaf spring units on the Chevrolet model, each consisting of two leaf springs, two pins, and one block. Draw

172

and cut out the eight leaf springs from rigid cardboard as shown in Diagram 31. Draw the spring design on both sides of each leaf spring, using pen and black drawing ink.

The parallel leaf springs of each unit are joined at each end by a pin. Cut the eight pins from large matchstick wood to the length given in Diagram 31. Paint the pins black. Place one of the leaf springs flat on your work surface and glue one pin lengthwise to each end. Place a second leaf spring directly above the first and glue it to the pins, sandwich fashion. Clamp the two ends of the spring unit with metal spring clips until the glue has completely hardened. Repeat for the remaining three spring units.

The chassis of the Chevrolet model rests on four blocks on top of the leaf spring units. These blocks lift the chassis the extra ¼ inch it needs in order for the leaf spring and wheel-axle units to be attached. Each block is made from two pieces of large matchstick wood, which are glued together along one long side. Cut the eight pieces to the length shown in Diagram 31, and glue each block together as indicated in the same diagram. Paint the four completed blocks black. Glue one block lengthwise to the top of each spring unit, the same distance from each end and edge to edge with one long side. See Assembly Diagram 31.

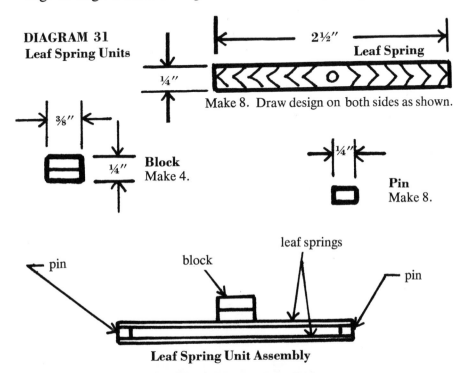

DIAGRAM 31
Leaf Spring Units

2½″   **Leaf Spring**

¼″

Make 8. Draw design on both sides as shown.

⅜″

¼″   **Block**
Make 4.

¼″

Pin
Make 8.

pin   block   leaf springs   pin

Leaf Spring Unit Assembly

Leaf Spring and Wheel-Axle Assembly

Turn the car model upside down and place a leaf spring unit, block side downward, in each corner of the chassis. Position the leaf spring units parallel to the sides of the chassis. Glue the blocks squarely in the chassis corners. Turn the car model right side up and let it rest on the blocks and springs on a flat surface until the glue hardens. As soon as the spring units are firmly attached to the chassis, the wheels and axles can be installed.

Turn the car model upside down once more. At each end of the chassis, slide the free end of one axle between the leaf springs of both end units and directly under the blocks. Put a generous amount of glue on the free ends of the axles and slide the two remaining wheels onto them. Position these wheels so they are also at right angles to the axles. Finally, adjust the axles so they are even with the front or back end of the chassis, and the wheels are the same distance from the right and left sides. The front axle should be even with the front edge of the blocks, and the rear axle should be even with the rear edge of the blocks. Put a generous amount of glue on the axles and attach them to both halves of each leaf spring unit. Look at the car model from several angles to make sure that the wheels are at perfect right angles to the chassis, and that you have attached the wheel axle and leaf spring units properly. Now your model should look like a real car.

Front Fenders (Diagram 32)

Draw and cut out the two front fenders, following Diagram 32. Use the color construction paper you have chosen for your model. Draw the line design as shown on one side of each fender, using pen and black drawing ink. Be sure to draw the design on opposite sides for the right and left fenders. Fold along the dotted lines carefully, folding toward the decorated side.

The forward portion of the front fenders curves over the wheels as shown in the side view in Diagram 32. To form this shape, pull the underside of the front fenders lengthwise over the edge of your work surface or ruler to make the paper curl.

174

DIAGRAM 32
Front Fenders

Make 2.

Draw line design as shown
on opposite sides of each fender.

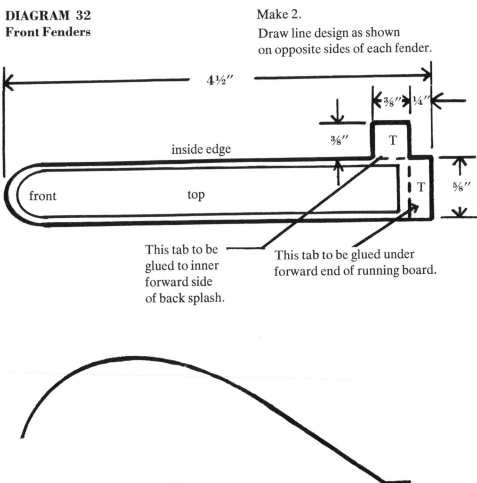

Side View of Front Fender

The front fenders are attached to the chassis by their two gluing tabs. Glue the tab at the rear of each fender to the underside of the forward end of the running board. Glue the side tab to the inner forward side of the back splash. If you used good stiff construction paper, these two attachment points for the fenders should be enough to hold them in position.

Rear Fenders (Diagram 33)

The rear fenders are identical to the front fenders, except for their curved shape. Draw and cut out these two pieces as shown in Diagram 33. Use the same color construction paper you used for the front fenders. Draw the line design with pen and black drawing ink. Again, remember to draw on opposite sides for the right and left fenders. Fold the gluing tabs toward the decorated sides.

The rear fender's curve is not as sharp as the front fender's. Pull the rear portion of the rear fenders over your work surface or ruler edge to form the curve shown in the side view in Diagram 33. Glue the end gluing tab of each rear fender to the underside of the rear end of the running board. Glue the side fender tab to the inner side of the back splash, also at the rear end.

DIAGRAM 33
Rear Fenders

Make 2.
Draw line design as shown
on opposite sides of each fender.

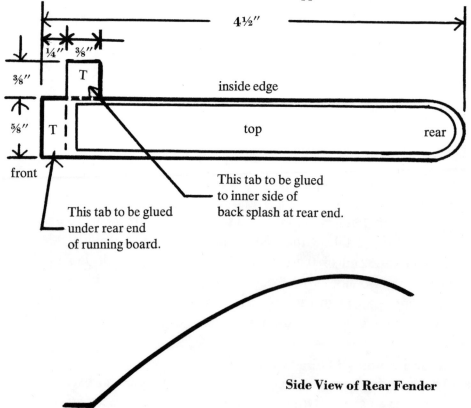

This tab to be glued
under rear end
of running board.

This tab to be glued
to inner side of
back splash at rear end.

Side View of Rear Fender

DIAGRAM 34
Spare Tire
Make 1.
Draw tire design
as shown on
both sides.

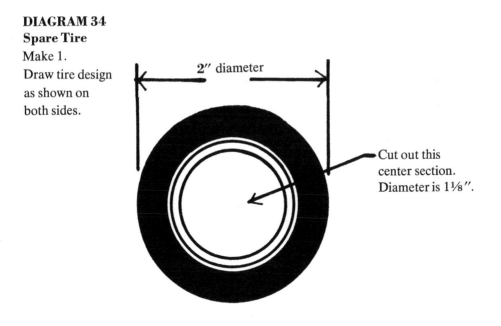

2″ diameter

Cut out this
center section.
Diameter is 1⅛″.

Spare Tire (Diagram 34)

The spare tire is the same as the other wheels of the Chevrolet model, except that its center portion is removed. Draw the spare tire on rigid cardboard as shown in Diagram 34. Cut it out along the outside edge only. Draw the tire and circle design on both sides of the wheel with pen and black drawing ink.

Removing the center part of the tire takes a little time and patience. Continue drawing the center circle of the tire with your compass until you have made a fairly deep impression in the cardboard. Then with the point of your sharp knife, cut along the compass track you have made. Press firmly on the knife but move slowly. If you try to cut too quickly, you may go off on an angle and ruin the circular shape of the cutout. Continue to cut with your knife until you feel that you have almost cut through the circle. Then, if you wish, turn the piece over and cut into the circular track on the reverse side. You may prefer to cut through on one side only. Either way you choose, the center portion should come free easily.

Spare Tire Holder (Diagram 35)

The spare tire is attached to the back of the model with an upside-down T-shaped holder. This consists of two simple rectangular pieces of rigid cardboard. Draw and cut out the pieces as shown in Diagram 35. Glue the pieces at right angles to one another as shown in Assembly Diagram 35. Paint the holder the color you have chosen for your model.

The spare tire holder is attached to the tail end of the chassis as shown in Diagram 35. Glue one end of the base of the holder to the underside of the chassis so it is the same distance from the right and left sides. Make sure the upright piece is parallel to the edge of the chassis.

Glue the spare tire to the holder at an angle so that the bottom portion of the tire rests on the rear end of the base. Glue the upper portion of the tire where it rests on the toolbox. See the photograph of the finished model on page 169.

DIAGRAM 35
Spare Tire Holder

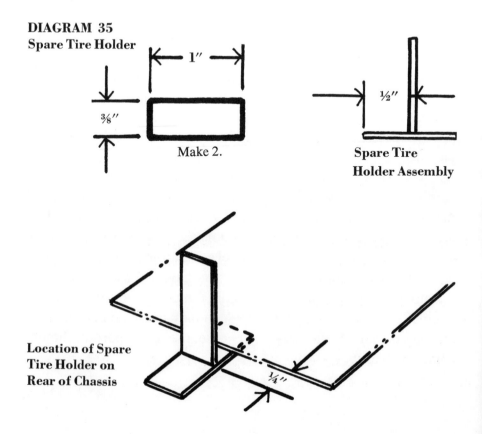

1"

3/8"

Make 2.

1/2"

**Spare Tire
Holder Assembly**

**Location of Spare
Tire Holder on
Rear of Chassis**

1/4"

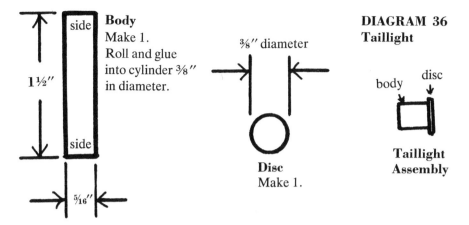

DIAGRAM 36
Taillight

Body
Make 1.
Roll and glue into cylinder ⅜″ in diameter.

⅜″ diameter

side

1½″

side

⅝₆″

Disc
Make 1.

body   disc

**Taillight
Assembly**

Taillight (Diagram 36)

This Chevrolet model has one taillight, which is attached to the back of the toolbox near the center of the spare tire. Draw and cut out the body of the taillight from black construction paper as shown in Diagram 36. Pull the piece lengthwise over the edge of your work surface or ruler to curl it. Roll it into a cylinder ¼ inch in diameter. If the ends seem to overlap too much for gluing, trim one of them with your scissors. Slide a pencil through the cylinder for support and glue the overlapping ends closed.

Draw and cut out the taillight disc, as shown in Diagram 36, from the brightest red construction paper you can find. Glue the disc to one end of the taillight body, as shown in Assembly Diagram 36. Glue the disc end of the taillight to the center of the top edge of the spare tire holder and the open end of the taillight to the toolbox. See the photograph of the finished model on page 169.

Front and Rear License Plates (Diagram 37)

The model of the 1915 Chevrolet must have license plates, of course! The two plates are identical. Draw and cut out these pieces from rigid cardboard as shown in Diagram 37. Draw the numbers as shown on one side of each plate with pen and black drawing ink.

Only the rear license plate is attached at this stage. The front plate will be added after the headlights have been installed. Place

179

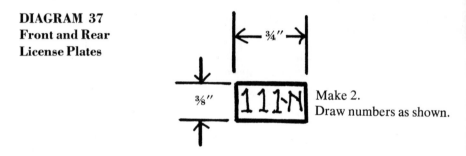

**DIAGRAM 37
Front and Rear
License Plates**

¾"

⅜"

1 1 1 N

Make 2.
Draw numbers as shown.

the rear license plate at an angle directly under the taillight. Glue the center of its top edge to the taillight disc and the upright of the spare tire holder. Glue the lower corners of the plate where they rest on the spare tire. See the photograph of the finished model on page 169.

Windshield Light (Diagram 38)

On the driver's side of the Chevrolet, there was a light on the outside edge of the windshield.

Draw and cut out the body of the windshield light as shown in Diagram 38. Use the color construction paper you have chosen for your model. Draw the piece lengthwise over the edge of your work surface or ruler to curl it. Roll it into a cylinder ¼ inch in diameter. If the overlapped ends make gluing difficult, trim one of them with your scissors. Glue the cylinder closed, using a pencil inside the tube as a support.

The front of the windshield light is a disc with several circles drawn on it to indicate a rim and glass. Draw and cut out the front disc from white construction paper as shown in Diagram 38. Draw the circles as indicated on one side of the disc with pen and black drawing ink. Glue the disc, pattern side outward, to either end of the light body. This end is now the front end of the windshield light.

The back end of the windshield light is covered with a disc with the same diameter as the body of the windshield light. Draw and cut out the back disc as shown in Diagram 38, using the same color construction paper you used for the light body. Glue the disc to the edge of the open end of the body.

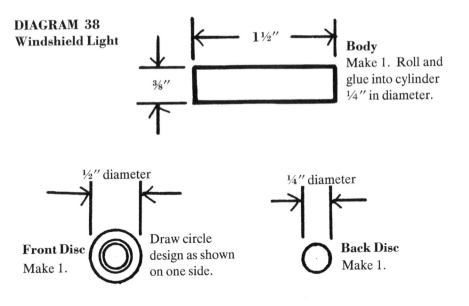

DIAGRAM 38
Windshield Light

1½″

3/8″

Body
Make 1. Roll and glue into cylinder ¼″ in diameter.

½″ diameter

¼″ diameter

Front Disc
Make 1.

Draw circle design as shown on one side.

Back Disc
Make 1.

Before you glue the completed light in position, turn the car model on its right side. Place the windshield light body at the center of the left side of the windshield frame, light side facing forward. Use the string which divides the frame in half to check the light's position. Glue the body to the windshield, letting the glue dry for a few minutes and become tacky before pressing the light to the frame. See the photograph of the finished model on page 133.

Horn (Diagram 39)

The horn of the Chevrolet is attached to the front end of the left running board.

Draw and cut out the horn body from black construction paper as shown in Diagram 39. Pull it lengthwise over the edge of your work surface or ruler to curl it. Then roll the body into a cylinder 3/8 inch in diameter. Trim one of the ends if the overlapping seems excessive. Insert a pencil in the cylinder for support and press the glued, overlapping ends together.

One end of the horn body cylinder is covered with a black construction paper disc. Draw and cut out this part as shown in

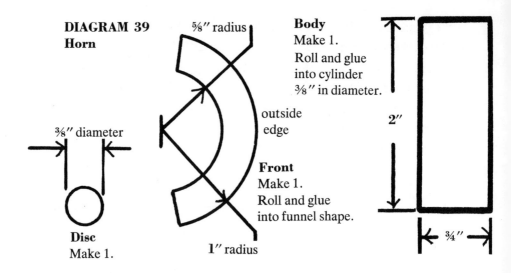

DIAGRAM 39
Horn

⅝″ radius

Body
Make 1.
Roll and glue
into cylinder
⅜″ in diameter.

outside
edge

⅜″ diameter

2″

Front
Make 1.
Roll and glue
into funnel shape.

Disc
Make 1.

1″ radius

¾″

Diagram 39. Glue the disc to either end of the horn body. This end is now the back end of the body.

Extending from the front end of the horn body is a funnel shape. Draw and cut out this part as shown in Diagram 39. Use the color construction paper you have chosen for your model. Draw the piece over the edge of your work surface or ruler to curl the paper and make it easier to shape. Bring the ends together to form a funnel which is slightly less than ⅜ inch in diameter at its small end. Make sure that the small end of the funnel fits just inside the front end of the horn body. Then glue the overlapping funnel ends closed. Attach the funnel to the horn body by putting glue around the inside open edge of the body piece and pressing the small end of the funnel onto the glued edge.

Place the completed horn on the forward end of the left running board, with the funnel end facing forward and the right side resting against the back splash. Put a little glue on the horn where it touches the running board and the back splash, and press in place.

Headlights (Diagram 40)

The two headlights of the Chevrolet model are assembled in

182

exactly the same way as the other lights you have already constructed. Draw and cut out the headlight bodies as shown in
Diagram 40. Use the color construction paper you have chosen
for your model. Draw the pieces lengthwise over your work surface or ruler edge to curl. Then roll the pieces into cylinders ½
inch in diameter. Trim any excess overlap and glue the ends
together, sliding a pencil inside the cylinders for support.

A white construction paper disc is attached to the front end
of each headlight. Draw and cut out these pieces as shown in
Diagram 40. Draw the circle design representing the headlight
glass and rim on one side of each disc, using pen and black ink.
Glue the plain side of the discs to either end of the cylinder bodies
so the overhang is the same all around. It is important that the
cylinders be centered on the discs so the headlights will be even
when they are attached to the front of the model.

The headlights are covered at the back end by discs which have
the same diameter as the headlight bodies. Draw and cut out these

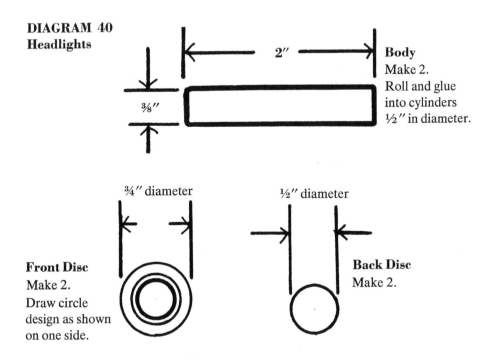

DIAGRAM 40
Headlights

2″ **Body**
Make 2.
Roll and glue
into cylinders
½″ in diameter.

⅜″

¾″ diameter

½″ diameter

Front Disc
Make 2.
Draw circle
design as shown
on one side.

Back Disc
Make 2.

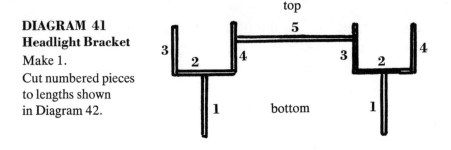

DIAGRAM 41
Headlight Bracket
Make 1.
Cut numbered pieces
to lengths shown
in Diagram 42.

top

5

3   2   4   3   2   4

1   bottom   1

pieces as shown in Diagram 40. Use the same color construction paper you used for the bodies of the headlights. Glue a disc to the back end of each headlight body. Set the headlights aside until their bracket is complete.

Headlight Bracket (Diagrams 41-42)

The headlight bracket is made from lengths of round toothpick. It is assembled and glued in the same way as the side roof frames.

Draw the pattern of the completed bracket as shown in Diagram 41 on a flat wood surface or shiny cardboard. Cut the round toothpicks to the lengths given for each numbered piece in Diagram 42. Place these lengths in position on the drawn pattern and glue the bracket together at each joint. Let the bracket dry for about half an hour. Then slide the flat side of your knife under each joint, twisting the knife gently to free the joints from the wood or cardboard surface. Look at the bracket from both sides and adjust any pieces that are not in a straight line. Put the bracket aside to let the glue harden permanently.

Headlight Bracket Supports (Diagram 42)

The headlight bracket is attached to the front end of the car model by two supports. Draw and cut out these supports from rigid cardboard as shown in Diagram 42. Paint them the same color as the chassis.

Measure the distance between the downward extending legs of the headlight bracket. Turn the car model upside down and mark

184

this measurement on the front end of the chassis, making sure the two points are the same distance from the sides. Place one support on each point so that half its length extends forward from the front end of the chassis. Check to make sure that the supports are even with the sides of the chassis, and that they are the correct distance apart to firmly support the bracket legs. Glue the supports in place.

As soon as the supports are firmly attached, the headlight bracket can be glued to them. Turn the car model right side up and put a generous amount of glue on the top side of each support. Let the glue dry for a few minutes and become tacky. Then press the legs of the bracket into the glue. The bracket should stand upright by itself. Before the glue hardens permanently, make certain that the bracket is in a perfectly vertical position and that it does not lean forward or backward toward the radiator.

DIAGRAM 42

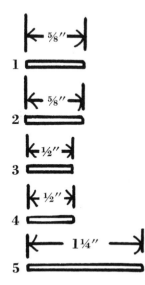

Headlight Bracket Lengths

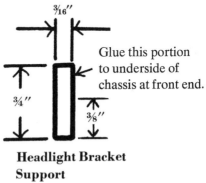

Glue this portion to underside of chassis at front end.

Headlight Bracket Support
Make 2.

Installing the Headlights

Once the legs are securely attached, the headlights can be glued to the U-shaped sections of the headlight bracket. One by one, place the headlights on the bracket as shown in the photograph of the finished model on page 151. Put a generous amount of glue on the points where the headlights touch the bracket. Let the glue become tacky before pressing the headlights in position. Make sure the headlights are parallel to one another and do not lean forward or backward. You will probably have to hold them for a few minutes until they can stay perfectly upright.

Installing the Front License Plate

Once the headlights and bracket are installed, you can attach the the front license plate. It is glued to the horizontal length of the bracket which connects the two headlight supports. Glue the top edge of the license plate to the underside of the horizontal piece. See the photograph of the finished model on page 133.

DIAGRAM 43

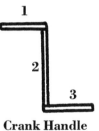

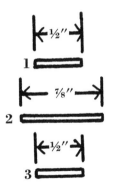

Crank Handle
Make 1.
Cut numbered pieces
to lengths shown.

Crank Handle (Diagram 43)

The last part to be added to the Chevrolet model is the crank handle. It is made from three pieces of round toothpick cut to the numbered lengths shown in Diagram 43. Cut and assemble the lengths as shown in the pattern in Diagram 43. It is not necessary to draw a pattern since there are only three lengths involved. While the pieces are still lying flat, glue the crank handle together at its two joints. After it is firmly glued, paint the crank handle black.

One end of the crank handle is glued in the hole in the bottom edge of the radiator that was made at the beginning of this model's construction. Put a generous amount of glue on the end to be inserted and push about ⅛ inch of the glued end into the hole. Turn the crank handle to one side for a more realistic appearance. See the photograph of the finished model on page 133.

This completes your model of the 1915 Chevrolet. If you worked carefully and accurately, your car model should be a strong contender for top honors at any antique car rally!

Glossary

Axle—A horizontal rod to which the wheels and car body are attached.

Back Splash—A vertical panel closing the opening between the car body and the running board.

Bulkhead—A rigid vertical support fixed at various points on the chassis, which provides an attachment for the body covering, giving it form and strength.

Carriage Lamp—Before battery-powered lights were developed, early cars had oil lamps. These were similar to lamps on horse-drawn carriages, hence the name.

Chassis—A frame or base to which the body and other car parts are attached.

Cowling—A curved covering section between the car body and motor compartment.

Crank Handle—Before the invention of the self-started car, motors had to be started by hand cranking. A handle jutting forward from the lower part of the radiator was used.

Dashboard—A rigid structure at the front of the driver's compartment to which instruments, like the mileage gauge and oil gauge, are attached.

Foot Board—The slanted, forward part of the floor in the driver's section.

Leaf Spring—On real cars, this is a spring consisting of a series of overlapping metal plates. Springs are the connecting link between the car body and the axles.

Radiator—A water-filled unit at the front of the motor compartment. On gasoline-powered cars, it helps to keep the engine cool.

Running Board—A step on the side of a car for the driver and passenger to climb into the vehicle. Modern autos do not have them.

Steering Lever—On very early cars, drivers steered with a lever. This was a short horizontal bar fixed to a shaft which was connected to the front axle.

Wheel Box—A box-shaped unit on the car models which is glued to the inner side of the wheels. It serves as a means for connecting the wheels to the axle.

Further Reading

Automobile Manufacturers Association, Inc. *Automobiles of America*. Detroit: Wayne State University Press, 1968.

Clymer, Floyd. *Those Wonderful Old Automobiles*. New York: Bonanza Books (Div. of Crown Publishers, Inc.), 1953.

Editors of Automobile Quarterly. *The American Car Since 1775*. New York: Automobile Quarterly, Inc. 1971.

Ross, Frank, Jr. *Historic Racing Car Models*. New York: Lothrop, Lee & Shepard Company, 1976.

Stein, Ralph. *The Treasury of the Automobile*. New York: Golden Press-Ridge Press, Inc., 1961.

Index

*indicates photo

Baby Grand, 134

cardboard, rigid, 9–10, 14
Chevrolet (1915), 7, 13, 135
Chevrolet Company, 134–135
Chevrolet, Louis, 133–134
Chevrolet model, 133*, 135–187,
    151*, 169*, 186*
compass, 12, 14
crayon, 10, 11
curve, plastic, 12
Curved Dash Olds (1902), 18–19
Curved Dash Olds model, 17*,
    19–50, 44*, 49*

Durant, W. C., 134

Ford, Henry, 18
"490" car, 134–135

General Motors Corporation, 19,
    134, 135
glue, 9, 10, 11–12

hammer, 12, 15

ink, India, 10, 11

knife, 11, 14, 15

Locomobile Company, 87

Marriott, Fred, 88

mass production, 18, 87
matchsticks, 10, 12, 15
materials, 9–11

nail, 12

oaktag, 9
Olds Motor Works, 18
Olds, Ransom Eli, 17–19

paintbrush, 12
paints, poster, 11
paper, construction, 9
pen, drawing, 12
pencils, 12

REO, 19
Royal Mail Roadster, 135
ruler, 12

scissors, 11
Stanley Steamer (1911), 13, 88
Stanley Steamer model, 86*, 89–
    132, 111*, 118*
straws, drinking, 10, 15

tape, masking, 12, 14
thread, 10
tools, 11–12
toothpicks, 10, 12
tweezers, 12

191

Waverley Stanhope Electric (1909), 13, 51–53
Waverley Stanhope Electric model, 51*, 53–85, 68*, 78*

White Motor Company, 19
wire, 11
wood, block of, 12, 15